30·DAY
JOB PROMOTION

build a powerful promotion plan in a month

SUSAN BRITTON WHITCOMB

Also in JIST's Help in a Hurry Series

- *Next-Day Salary Negotiation*
- *Same-Day Resume*
- *Next-Day Job Interview*
- *15-Minute Cover Letter*
- *Seven-Step Job Search*

jist
Works
America's Career Publisher™

PART OF JIST'S HELP IN A HURRY™ SERIES

30•DAY JOB PROMOTION

© 2008 by Susan Britton Whitcomb

Published by JIST Works, an imprint of JIST Publishing, Inc.
8902 Otis Avenue
Indianapolis, IN 46216-1033
Phone: 1-800-648-JIST   Fax: 1-800-JIST-FAX   E-mail: info@jist.com

Visit our Web site at www.jist.com for information on JIST, free job search tips, book chapters, and ordering instructions for our many products!

Quantity discounts are available for JIST books. Have future editions of JIST books automatically delivered to you on publication through our convenient standing order program. Please call our Sales Department at 1-800-648-5478 for a free catalog and more information.

Trade Product Manager: Lori Cates Hand
Interior Designer: Aleata Howard
Page Layout: Trudy Coler
Cover Designer: Katy Bodenmiller
Proofreaders: Paula Lowell, Jeanne Clark
Indexer: Cheryl Lenser

Printed in the United States of America
12 11 10 09 08 07   9 8 7 6 5 4 3 2 1

Library of Congress Cataloging-in-Publication data

Whitcomb, Susan Britton, 1957-
    30-day job promotion : build a powerful promotion plan in a month / Susan Britton
    Whitcomb.
              p. cm. -- (JIST's help in a hurry series)
    Includes bibliographical references and index.
    ISBN-13: 978-1-59357-447-5 (alk. paper)
    1. Promotions. 2. Career development. I. Title. II. Title: Thirty day job
    promotion.
    HF5549.5.P7W47 2008
    650.14--dc22
                                    2007019300

ISBN 978-1-59357-447-5

About This Book

What stands in the way of your being enthusiastically engaged and radically rewarded in your career? You might say it's a lack of openings, or a personality clash with your boss, or office politics, or any number of challenges that prevent you from moving forward with your current employer.

This book is for all who want to truly take charge of their career—to shift from "victim" to "victorious" or move from "stuck" to "steadfast" in the pursuit of your goals and dreams. *30-Day Job Promotion* is designed to give you a powerful promotion plan, with strategies to turn obstacles into opportunities and set you on an irrevocable course of career progress.

In the first chapter, you'll uncover your motives for getting promoted and learn the top 10 characteristics of promotable people. You'll also get clear on your company's situation and how that might impact your promotion, as well as identify your position target and elements of the ideal fit.

In chapter 2, you'll discover the importance of timing and put together a 30-day plan to proactively prepare yourself for promotion. Yes, there may be factors out of your control that will require patience on your part, but you'll also learn how to avoid common mistakes and expedite the promotion process.

Chapter 3 outlines the "10 Commandments" of Career Success and gives you the opportunity to score yourself on 150 items that impact your promotability factor. In chapter 4, you learn the "T.A.L.K."-it-out formula for having crucial career conversations with the people who have the power to promote you. Chapter 5 offers strategies to circumvent common roadblocks and covers everything from a difficult relationship with your boss to office politics.

In chapter 6, you'll learn how to get paid for the work you really do, with a 10-step process for negotiating salary. Chapter 7 offers inspiring, real-life success stories of people from many walks of life who landed their dream promotions.

In the appendices, you'll find assessments to give you a competitive edge, worksheets to help you identify your value, resume and position proposal examples, a survey to gauge your communication skills, and a listing of coaches who contributed success stories to chapter 7 (you'll find it helpful to work with a coach on your promotion campaign).

May your success be significant!

Susan Britton Whitcomb

Acknowledgments

Special thanks to Kathy Bitschenauer of New Pathways Career Coaching, who was instrumental in helping shape the content of this book—I appreciate all those midnight e-mail responses. To Robyn Feldberg of Abundant Success Career Services, heartfelt thanks for bringing life to the success stories—your commitment to seeing people succeed is inspiring! To my coach, Judy Santos, thanks for helping make book #5 a reality—your partnership, wisdom, insight, and prayers are priceless. And to my dad John Britton, thanks for weathering those decades of farming so that I'd have a wealth of metaphors for success in life!

There's a long list of people whose thought leadership has added value to this book—thank you to Nancy Branton, Dr. Ronald Page, Dale Kurow, Jane Cranston, Mixie Kingman Eddy, Deb Dib, Louise Kursmark, Wendy Enelow, and many others who have not only deepened the content of this book, but enhanced my life as well. And, recognition is due the team at JIST, with special acknowledgement of my editor Lori Cates Hand—you are the epitome of career success, forever "controlling the controllables" and using your talents to enrich the world.

Contents

Chapter 1

What Will a Promotion Mean to You?

What prompted you to pick up this book?

- Are you feeling unappreciated at work?
- Do you believe you aren't getting paid enough?
- Does your job lack the challenges you want?

Many people start to dust off their resume in search of greener pastures when these thoughts come. And come, they do! More than 75 percent of employees reported intentions to leave their job, according to a 2006 job retention poll conducted by the Society for Human Resource Management and the *Wall Street Journal's* CareerJournal.com.

A full-scale job search is a serious undertaking that, when done right, requires a great deal of work and a certain amount of risk. What many fail to recognize is that those greener pastures are often located in their own back yard...with their current employer. In other words, you have the power to create greener pastures by watering your own back yard!

Today, career management is an entrepreneurial game. As a "career entrepreneur," you are in charge of making your career grow and prosper. You, and no one else—not your human resources director, your mentor, your manager, your colleagues, or your coach. Smart careerists are able to thoroughly leverage the opportunities "hiding" in plain view. You'll learn how to do just that in short order. First, let's look at what a promotion will mean to you.

A Dozen Reasons to Get Promoted

If you ask a dozen people what a promotion means to them, you'll likely get as many answers! For example:

1. More money
2. An impressive title or perks

3. New types of projects to work on

4. A chance to work with people you admire and respect

5. A greater sense of purpose or significance

6. More responsibility, recognition, or respect

7. The approval of friends/family/peers/professional associates

8. Fewer hate-to-do responsibilities and more love-to-do responsibilities

9. A better work schedule, perhaps including some telecommuting

10. New challenges to take on and skills to learn

11. A stepping stone toward a long-term ambition

12. A sense of accomplishment

Later in this chapter, you'll identify specifically what a promotion means to you and how your life will change as a result. In the meantime, if you look closely at the Dozen Reasons just listed, you'll likely see a common theme that underlies each of the factors:

Forward Progress

As a human being, you were wired from birth to make progress. If you're not learning and stretching, you'll eventually become stifled and stagnant. Just as plants need the right conditions to flourish, you need the right conditions to thrive, or a piece of you will wither and die. A healthy career involves a continuous process of stretching and growing…and not just from an intellectual perspective, such as learning the latest software or acquiring new industry knowledge.

A deeper, more meaningful level of progress comes when you master the "soft" skills, sometimes referred to as your emotional intelligence (EI) or social intelligence. Those with high EI are good at managing their emotions, dealing with stress, displaying empathy, seeing things from others' perspectives, and remaining optimistic despite formidable odds. Part of your promotability rests on EI, which is comprised of skills such as self-awareness, self-management, social awareness, and relationship management. In fact, experts say that, for certain professions, up to 45 percent of work success is dependent on EI.

Be Open to Surprises

One of my coaching clients, "Winnie," offered insights on her quest for promotion: "Looking back, I realize that this itch to get a new position was not just about getting promoted—it was about moving forward and seeing opportunities that I didn't realize were there. There was something almost divine about it, taking me out of tunnel vision and helping me see the bigger picture.

"I had tried for years to get promoted in my company. After working with my coach, an amazing series of events opened up. I had the opportunity to return to school and start a second master's degree (after already having my doctorate), but this particular program will allow me to do what I want to do long-term. In the registration process, doors flew open! I was given special consideration, registering for the program in four days (of course, the paperwork still needs to be turned in) and starting classes the following week. After getting the feel for what it's like to be back in school and handling my job, I realized I could still do more.

"That gave me the confidence to submit a proposal for a new position involving the creation of a Web-based employee development program. The proposal was well received by the director and we're now in discussions with the CIO. I feel like I'm really making progress in my career."

Meaningful progress is also linked to getting your needs met. As you consider what forward progress means to you, think about how your "career needs" have changed over time. Everyone has unique needs. Some of those needs are extremely basic and common to us all, such as feeding and watering ourselves on a daily basis. Your body has a clear system to signal hunger or thirst—your stomach growls and your mouth gets dry. You also have higher-level needs that are less readily apparent, such as the need to be imaginative on the job or the need to have appreciation expressed for your work. Unfortunately, the signaling mechanism for these career-related needs is not always so clear. Instead of a growling stomach to signal hunger, you might have a growling temper, a lack of energy, or a sick feeling in your stomach on Monday mornings to signal that your career-related needs are not being met.

What Do You Really Need from Your Career?

In an earlier book, *Job Search Magic*, I described how needs are key to understanding motivation. Psychologist Abraham Maslow developed a

Hierarchy of Needs model in the 1940s that is acknowledged today by both psychologists and business leaders as fundamental to understanding human motivation. The original hierarchy presents five basic levels of need:

1. Physiological: Food, water, shelter, sleep

2. Safety: Security, freedom from fear

3. Belonging and Love: Friends, family, spouse, affection, relationships

4. Self-Esteem: Achievement, mastery, recognition, respect

5. Self-Actualization: Pursuit of inner talents, creativity, fulfillment

The theory states that people are motivated by unsatisfied needs. The lower-level needs (physiological and safety) must be met before a person is motivated to satisfy a higher need (self-esteem and self-actualization). For example, someone who has not eaten for three days (level-1 needs) will not be motivated to pursue achievement and mastery (level-4 needs).

I have identified some career counterparts to Maslow's model, as table 1.1 illustrates.

Table 1.1: Hierarchy of Career Needs	
Maslow's Original Hierarchy of Needs	*Career Counterparts*
Level 1: Physiological (food, water, shelter, sleep)	Basic paycheck, manageable work hours
Level 2: Safety (security, stability, freedom from fear)	Work environment free of violence, abuse, pollutants, danger, or continual threat of job loss
Level 3: Belonging and Love (friends, family, spouse, affection, relationships)	Organizational culture and camaraderie; relationships with supervisor, peers, co-workers, customers, even vendors/suppliers
Level 4: Esteem (achievement, mastery, recognition, respect)	Impressive title; awards; a sense of appreciation received through praise/thanks, promotions, level of responsibility or authority, upper-range salary, perks; a belief that company policy is fair and respectful of the employee

Level 5: Self-Actualization (pursuit of inner talents, creativity, fulfillment)	Personal growth; full utilization of talents on the job; you are able to be authentic and bring the essence of yourself the job; there is enthusiastic engagement in work; work is passion-driven; career activity is a means to fulfilling one's destiny; use of talents may even be sacrificial for a greater good; there is contribution to a living legacy that leaves a positive social, environmental, or spiritual impact

Maslow later added to his model Cognitive and Aesthetic needs, to know and understand and to have symmetry, order, and beauty, respectively. These come before Self-Actualization. He also added the level of Transcendence as a final level, which goes beyond Self-Actualization. With Transcendence, the individual has a need to connect with something beyond self or to help others reach their potential. These concepts are consistent with the theme of pursuing purpose-driven work and leaving a legacy.

CAREER NEEDS

Take a moment now to determine which of the levels on the hierarchy of career needs that you identify with most. In your current situation, are you at Level 1 or 2 (at a minimum), just earning a basic paycheck and working in an environment that's safe? Are you at Level 3, where there's a sense of belonging, with organizational camaraderie amongst coworkers? Perhaps it's Level 4, where you're earning the awards and rewards that are important to you at this point in your life. Or, maybe you identify with Level 5 and, through your work, are creating a living legacy. You can move up or down on the levels, depending on your work circumstances.

From the items, list the Level of Needs and the Career Counterparts that are being met in your current position:

_____

_____

(continued)

(continued)

Next, take a moment to decide which of the career needs are important for you in your next career opportunity:

_____

_____

_____

_____

_____

Interestingly, the highest level on Maslow's Hierarchy of Needs, Self-Actualization, has also been identified by EI researcher Reuven Bar-On, Ph.D., as the most important of all 15 EI factors in career success.

What's Driving You?

It's also important to get to the root of why you want to be promoted—your motivation. When you're clear on why you want something and what it will mean to your life, you'll have more focus and energy to go after it. Although the Dozen Reasons in the previous section presents a number of ideas, conversations with countless managers seem to point to three primal motivations:

1. **Money:** The desire for higher salary is not a bad thing, especially if your employer has been paying you below industry standards or the norm for your geographic area (read more on getting what you're worth in chapter 6 on salary). Just make sure that money isn't your only motivator.

Tip: *Leave any personal financial woes out of the picture when discussing a promotion with your manager. One retail store manager related the incident of an indiscreet employee who asked for a promotion by leading off with, "I'm having trouble making rent." Needless to say, it didn't set the stage for favorable future conversations!*

Reality check: It's unlikely that you'll go from rags to riches with an internal promotion (a promotion inside your current organization). Much depends on the employer. At some companies, a promotion might mean a salary increase of 25 percent. However, many companies limit pay raises to approximately 5 percent per pay grade. If you work for an employer like this and salary is most important to you, weigh the option of moving to another organization.

> **Tip:** *Employers should have good reason to put you into roles that will satisfy your itch! The Gallup organization, in a survey on the impact of employee attitudes on business outcomes, noted that organizations where employees have above-average attitudes toward their work had 38 percent higher customer satisfaction scores, 22 percent higher productivity, and 27 percent higher profits.*

2. **Ego:** Many people have a healthy, well-balanced sense of confidence and self-esteem, which can include a desire to be recognized for their contributions. At the far end of the spectrum, however, are those who lean toward egoism, with an excessive concern about themselves and an overzealous desire to impress others—their primary motivation for making decisions is whether other people will think favorably about them.

Chris, a senior district manager for a national company who has made hundreds of hiring and promotion decisions, offered an interesting insight on this topic: "When it comes to wanting a promotion, I see ego, and not money, as the primary push for most people. Salary increases are often minimal with internal promotions. The prestige of the title means more to them than the paycheck."

As with motivator #1 (money), ego isn't necessarily a bad thing. It will serve you best when balanced with a concern for the common good, which brings us to motivator number three.

3. **Itch:** Itch is the desire to be more, learn more, and do more. It's the urge to stretch and grow. The hunger to create something new. The drive to contribute more significantly or leave a bigger mark on your corner of the world. Motivator #3, the itch, is the motivator that managers will be most impressed with. Altruistic in nature, it shows that you're interested in the company's overall success and not just your own. This will go far with your management team.

RATE YOURSELF

On a scale of 1 to 10 (1 being not at all true for me and 10 being very true for me), how would you rate your motivation on the three factors?

Money: _____

Ego: _____

Itch: _____

Are your motivators rooted solely in money or ego? _____

If this is the case, what would it take for you to make a shift to "itch," where the focus is less on you and more on the company?

_____

_____

_____

Top 10 Characteristics of Promotable People

What makes someone promotable? Having interviewed numerous managers and worked with hundreds of career-minded clients over the years, a clear pattern emerged. Those with the greatest promotability demonstrated a blend of hard skills and, more importantly, soft skills, as shown in figure 1.1.

These characteristics can be elaborated upon as follows:

- **Character:** Promotable people have earned a reputation as trustworthy, impeccably ethical, conscientious, and open-minded.

- **Confidence:** Promotable people take calculated risks, trust their instincts, are optimistic and courageous, and drive past any fears that might hold them back.

- **Communication:** Strong communication skills are common to promotable people; they speak with clarity and persuasion. Further, their presentation style is devoid of distractions with regard to appearance, dress, or habits.

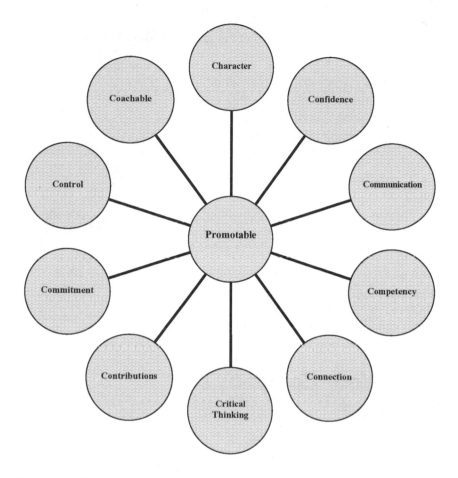

Figure 1.1: The 10 C's of Promotable People.

- **Competency:** Promotable people possess above-average position-specific abilities, industry knowledge, and technology skills.

- **Connection:** Promotable people have a charismatic ability to connect with others beyond the superficial level and create rapport with managers, internal constituencies, and customers.

- **Critical Thinking:** Able to see the "big picture" and always maintain a global organizational perspective, promotable people are able to grasp all facets of a situation and make the best decision.

- **Contributions:** Promotable people are results-oriented and make continual contributions that improve the company's bottom line.

- **Commitment:** Known for their perseverance, promotable people are committed and never give up.

- **Control:** Promotable people control their destiny (without controlling or manipulating others); they act to influence outcomes and do not lapse into powerlessness or passivity.

- **Coachable:** Promotable people are open to always learning more; in addition, they are able to implement coaching techniques to develop, grow, and manage others.

> **Tip:** *Be a learn-it-all! In her book* Mindset: The New Psychology of Success, *Stanford professor of psychology Carol S. Dweck, Ph.D., proposes that everyone has either a fixed mindset or a growth mindset. As the guest on a recent Thought Leader Teleforum hosted by Leadership CoachAcademy.com, Dr. Dweck shared that those with a fixed mindset are often know-it-alls, while those with a growth mindset are "learn-it-alls." Without a doubt, the learn-it-alls fit the characteristic of coachable.*

You may have all 10 of these promotability characteristics going for you (applause if you do!); however, there's another side to the promotion equation: the company and its situation.

Know Your Company's Situation

Promotion comes more easily when your employer and industry are on the upswing. Starbucks is currently opening more than 700 stores each quarter—that's eight new stores every day. Christine Deputy, Starbucks' VP of Global Staffing, noted its workforce has mushroomed from 25,000 to 130,000 employees in less than 10 years.

Compare Starbucks to the automotive industry, where automation, outsourcing, and globalization are forcing American workers to retool their skills and search for new niches. Ford recently announced layoffs of 30,000; GM, 50,000; and DaimlerChrysler, 13,000—a total reduction of 93,000.

Obviously, the state of your company and industry will factor into opportunities for promotion. These questions will help get a pulse on the state of your company:

- Is the company adding new employees?

- Is the company opening new locations?

- Is there an increase in workload? If so, is it attributable to an increase in sales?

- Has there been a reduction-in-force (RIF) or downsizing in the recent past?

- Is the organization in a financial position to sustain growth?

- Does the company have growth plans, status quo plans, or hunker-down-and-weather-the-storm plans?

- Does management appear stressed, with frequent mention of reducing expenses?

- Have others been promoted in the past couple of years? If so, how do your qualifications compare?

- What are the trends for your industry? Is growth, status quo, or decline predicted?

Resources for Fast-Growing Companies and Industries

America's Career InfoNet, funded by your tax dollars and the U.S. Department of Labor, lists America's fastest-growing industries (www.careerinfonet.org, click on Industry Information, and then Fastest-Growing Industries to see the list, "Top 50 Fastest-Growing Industries" as reported by the Bureau of Labor Statistics). Topping the list as this book went to press were educational support services, home health care services, and software publishers.

At the same Web site, you can find the highest-paying industries (start at www.careerinfonet.org, click on Industry Information, and then Highest-Paying Industries).

Want to see if your company is in growth mode? A great source is the Best List series published by Fortune. To learn what companies are on the list, go to

http://money.cnn.com/magazines/fortune/fortunefastestgrowing/2006/index.html

From there, you can search by state or stock returns.

Know Your Target

When considering your next promotion, you'll want to consider a few important questions:

- Will the next move be a stepping-stone position, something you plan to be in for a year or two? Or will it be your dream job, something you think you'd enjoy doing for as long as you can imagine?

- If it's a stepping stone, will the promotion show off your strengths and be something you're thoroughly passionate about? Or are you taking it merely because it will provide a core foundation of knowledge or experience necessary for future promotions? If the latter, what are the risks associated with doing so? How can you minimize these risks?

- If you are young in your career, what level of emotional intelligence will your managers expect of you in your next role? Making a move before you're ready could set you up for failure. Likewise, significant lack of skill sets or knowledge for the next position can also be a recipe for disaster. If you have an inkling this might be the case, discuss with your manager an in-between step to get your feet wet and give you some wins.

> **Tip:** *It's especially common in the sales industry for a top performer, because of stellar sales numbers, to be promoted from an individual contributor role to a sales management position. (Keep in mind that sales managers are evaluated partly on how many people they promote, so they're motivated to make promotions even when it might not be the wisest thing to do.) Managing people and handling a heavy administrative load requires a very different skill set than selling. Evaluate your strengths and think carefully about accepting such a promotion—you don't want to get in over your head.*

PROMOTION TARGET WORKSHEET

Use this worksheet to flesh out what your next promotion will really mean to you.

Title of position you're targeting:

_____

_____

_____

_____

Detailed job description of the new position:

_____

_____

_____

_____

_____

_____

_____

_____

_____

_____

_____

Bottom-line impact and value you'd be delivering in this position:

_____

_____

_____

Your motivation for wanting this:

_____

_____

_____

Where will this promotion take you in the long run?

_____

_____

_____

(continued)

(continued)

Ideally, how long would you like to stay in this position?

_____

What will this promotion bring to your life?

_____

_____

_____

How will your life change because of this?

_____

_____

_____

_____

Transport yourself into the future. It's one year from now and you're celebrating your anniversary of being hired for your new position. You're settled into the new job and delivering solid results. Describe a typical work day in detail, noting things like your level of confidence and self-esteem, the people with whom you regularly interact, the types of decisions you're making, what you're most proud of having accomplished this past year, and so on.

_____

_____

_____

_____

_____

_____

_____

_____

What thoughts and emotions come up for you as a result?

_____

_____

_____

Know Your Master F.I.T.™

Before proceeding with promotion plans, it's critical that you understand what type of position is the best fit for you. Table 1.2 describes in brief the Master F.I.T.™ model introduced in JIST's Magic series (in *Interview Magic* and *Job Search Magic*) that captures the six elements of a perfect career fit.

Table 1.2: Elements of the Master F.I.T.™

	F	I	T
External Variables	**Function** Function represents job titles and tasks; for example, titles such as accountant, copywriter, or customer service representative or tasks such as analyzing, planning, or writing. Although you're capable of doing a number of different functional jobs or tasks, you'll want to concentrate on your innate talents and skills, and favorite experiences.	**Industry/Interests** Industry refers to *where* you will apply your functional skills. Frequently, your functional interests can be used within a number of industries. For example, a customer service representative (Function) with a passion for organic products might target call centers (Industry) or retailers (Industry) that specialize in natural products (Interests).	**Things That Matter** Wouldn't it be wonderful if you could open the medicine cabinet each morning and pop a pill that would motivate you to go to work? That pill *does* exist! It takes the shape of having your values and needs met. In the "Things That Matter" category, you'll identify what's most important to you in your next position. Understanding and aligning your work with these values and needs can take your job from humdrum to fun, and your career from good to great!

	F	I	T
Internal Variables	**Fulfillment** Fulfillment is synonymous with purpose. Your career purpose can be described as being "radically rewarded and enthusiastically engaged in work that adds value to others." Your definition should capture the essence of how you will bring value to your employer, as well as how you will fulfill yourself. It's something you can intentionally look forward to on a Monday morning and say, "this is what I am committed to," as well as look back on Friday afternoon and say, "I have accomplished my purpose."	**Identity** Identity refers to how you see yourself—your internal self-image. It is the way in which you define yourself. What distinguishing character-istics do you want others to note in you? What do you *believe* you are capable of accomplishing? How do you want others to perceive you? Those who experience the greatest meaning and fulfillment in life work periodically to redefine themselves and move beyond their previously accepted limitations.	**Type** Type refers to your personality. You came wired-at-birth with four main personality preferences: where you focus your energy (your outer world or inner world); how you take in information (concretely or intuitively); how you make decisions (based on logic or feelings); and how you approach the world (in a planned or spontaneous manner).

If you're thinking that it will be a challenge to move into a position that ideally suits all six elements—your functional skills, ideal industry/interests,
things that matter, fulfilling purpose, evolving identity, and personality
type—don't be discouraged. It *is* possible; however, recognize that it is a
process of fine-tuning your career over time. Start by making sure you're
clear about the first-level elements—Function, Industry/Interests, and
Things That Matter—as you target new positions. Then, weave in your
second-level elements—Fulfillment, Identity, and Type—to take your career
to the next level. Use the worksheet that follows to fill in responses to each
of the elements. Your promotion should be enhancing one or more of the
Master F.I.T.™ elements.

CAREER "MASTER F.I.T.™" WORKSHEET

External "F.I.T." (the Easily Observable F.I.T.)	Internal "F.I.T." (the Less Observable, but Equally Important F.I.T.)
Function (<u>What</u> you *want and like* to do! What strengths/talents/skills/passions have you excelled at in the past? What would you like to learn to do? What job titles are associated with these functions? Conversely, what do you want to avoid? If there were one task you couldn't give up in your current career, what would it be? Job titles will often be associated with the <u>F</u>unction.)	**Fulfillment** (<u>Why</u> do you work? What is your purpose/cause/destiny? What difference do you want to make? How would you describe your living legacy? Why will this be rewarding?)
Industry (<u>Where</u> do you want to use your "function" skills? Where do your interests, knowledge, or experiences lie? What industries/companies/products do these interests represent? Conversely, what situations do you want to avoid?)	**Identity** (<u>Who</u> are you? Who are you becoming? What adjectives best describe your present and future you? How do you want others to perceive you? Who are your role models? Who have been your key supporters?)

Things That Matter (<u>Which</u> values and priorities— financial, work/lifestyle, environmental, intellectual, emotional, spiritual—must be present for you to be your best in your work?)

Type (<u>How</u> do you prefer to re-energize, take in information, make decisions, and orient your environment? For instance, are you more energized by people and things, or ideas and concepts? Do you primarily trust information that is tangible and concrete, or abstract and conceptual? Do you prefer to make decisions based on logic, or how they will affect people? Do you prefer an environment that is more controlled and predictable, or unstructured and variable? How do you learn best?)

It's obvious from this chapter that going for a promotion will take time and energy. When you're clear on the rewards, you'll know the investment will be worth it. Turn the page to step into your future!

Key Points: Chapter 1

- Uncover your motives for wanting a promotion.

- A promotion means different things to different people, such as more money; an impressive title; new types of projects to work on; a chance to work with people you admire and respect; a greater sense of purpose; more responsibility, recognition, or respect; approval of friends/family/ peers; fewer hate-to-do responsibilities and more love-to-do responsibilities; a better work schedule; new challenges; a stepping stone toward a long-term ambition; or a sense of accomplishment.

- Meaningful career progress means getting your needs met, so clarify the needs that are most important to you, which ones are currently being met, and which ones will be met in the new position.

- Money, ego, and itch (the desire to be more, learn more, and do more) are the three most common factors that drive a desire for promotion.

- The 10 characteristics of promotable people are character, confidence, communication, competency, connection, critical thinking, contributions, commitment, control, and coachability.

- Your company's financial situation, business strategy, and growth goals will impact your promotion opportunities.

- Get clear on your promotion target, including the title, responsibilities, bottom-line impact on the organization, what opportunities it might lead to long-term, how long you envision staying in this role, what the new position means for your future, and what it will bring to your life.

- Make sure the new position is a good "F.I.T.": It allows you to use your favorite Functional skills; it is in an Industry/Interest you enjoy; it aligns with the Things that Matter most to you; it brings meaningful Fulfillment; it is consistent with your Identity and how you see yourself or want others to perceive you; it complements your personality Type.

Chapter 2

Timing Is Everything!

This book is designed to help you do all the things you need to do within 30 days to position yourself for promotion. That means

- Having courageous conversations with your boss
- Creating new job descriptions or position proposals
- Polishing up your internal resume
- Writing before-after-and-beyond position descriptions and "Competency and Contributions" addenda (see chapter 4)
- Preparing strategically for performance evaluations
- Researching salary trends to better understand your market value, and so on

Of course, depending on your circumstances, you may do some, all, or more than what's briefly listed here. However, there's no way to guarantee that you will be promoted within 30 days! As the old saying goes, "Timing is everything." Of course, you'll learn some great strategies to create momentum, but there may also be times when you have to wait patiently (all the while continuing to deliver stellar results in your existing role).

As you follow the wisdom in this book, your goal should be to cultivate the ground and plant seeds with your manager so that you are top-of-mind when new opportunities present themselves.

The Importance of Timing

My father and brothers are third- and fourth-generation farmers who grow cotton in Central California. They know quite a bit about bringing in a harvest. To help you understand the importance of timing as it relates to sowing and reaping, here's a crash course in growing cotton, courtesy of my father John Britton's lifetime in cotton farming.

During late October or November, six months before seed can even go into the ground, the fields are cultivated with a "ripper" to break up dirt clods. They're then disked by a tractor to create bed-rows. In February, the fields are pre-irrigated. In mid-March, the ground is worked again and carefully monitored for temperature. Five consecutive days of 55-degree temperatures, exactly six inches below the surface, is the prerequisite for planting. If it's too cold, the seed won't germinate. Planting usually starts around mid-April. The seed is "planted to moisture," meaning 1.25 to 1.5 inches deep, to take advantage of the pre-irrigation. If the seed is planted too shallow, it will sprout but wither because the tap root won't be able to reach the moisture. If planted too deep, your only hope is a weather forecast that promises warmer-than-expected temperatures.

Within 7 to 10 days of planting, the tips break the surface of the soil. It's a beautiful sight to see acre after acre of this lush, gorgeous green. It's not unusual, however, to have to replant, as Mother Nature often has her own agenda. Even when the plant is off to a good start, it still needs one or two applications of fertilizer.

Cotton can grow seven to eight feet tall. But when it does, the plant sends all its energy into growing tall instead of producing the important bolls containing the actual fiber. To manage growth in organic cotton crops, a machine trims the tops to stunt the plant's growth. Of course, fertilizer is also necessary, and the fields must be irrigated four or five times over the course of June, July, and August, especially in very hot climates. Finally in mid-October, the cotton is ready for harvest.

I've just described a one-year cycle, from pre-work and pre-irrigation to planting, fertilizing, trimming, irrigating, and harvesting. It's likely your promotion won't take that long, but you can see the analogy. The fall/winter pre-work and pre-irrigation can represent the years of time you've already put in with your current employer, paying your dues. In the spring you plant seeds, paying attention to when the "temperature" is right by watching for strategic timing and the mood of your boss, the department, and the organization as a whole. Your promotion campaign will require extra watering to build trust with those who have the authority to promote you (or get on their radar screen if you don't have regular access to them).

There may be times when you feel as though you've been painfully pruned and frustratingly "fertilized," when in reality this can channel you to focus on producing the results that are most important for your career.

Although the promotion cycle may not be precise from situation to situation, the good news is that you're guaranteed a harvest. It's the proverbial law of sowing and reaping. Just make sure you're sowing good seed and waiting for a fully mature crop before harvesting.

Mistakes to Avoid

As you learned from the farming metaphor, one of the mistakes you'll want to avoid is pushing your manager too hard or too fast. If your manager feels rushed or pressured, it can break trust.

In general, stay clear of these additional faux pas when it comes to going for a promotion:

- **Overusing the terms "my career" or "promotion" in your discussions with your manager.** Language such as "I'm committed to being a part of the company's continued growth and success" is often more palatable than "I'd like to get promoted."

- **Going for too big a jump in responsibilities too soon.** For example, a junior programmer for a software-development company learned that a senior engineer was leaving for a new opportunity. The junior programmer marched into the director's office with a bulleted list of why she should be promoted to the senior engineer's position, but her plan backfired. In the director's eyes, it was too far a stretch. The junior programmer ended up with no promotion, when she might have landed some additional responsibility with an engineering title had she used a strategy that allowed for smaller steps.

> **Tip:** One Starbucks manager and district trainer described the timing factor this way: "It's music to my ears when an employee wants to be promoted and says it in a manner that doesn't put pressure on the relationship. I had one employee tell me, 'If you want to promote me, I'm more than ready, willing, and available to grow with the company; I also know you need great people out front with customers, so, until that time, I'm here for you with a 110 percent effort.' I promoted this particular employee in less than two months!"

- **Bugging your manager with too-frequent reminders of wanting to be promoted.** If, during your "career conversation" with your manager, you've been completely clear about your expectations and your manager has openly discussed what you need to do to move forward, reminders shouldn't be necessary. Just be sure you have calendared a time in the weeks or months to come to revisit the topic with your manager. In the meantime, work with excellence and optimism.

- **Begging for a promotion because of financial pressures.** Managers and business owners tend to take the attitude that you knew what the job paid when you took it and it's up to you to live within your income.

- **Pouting or grousing** because you haven't gotten promoted as quickly as you'd like. Act like an adult!

- **Whining or demanding that you be promoted** because you're envious or frustrated that someone else on your team got promoted. You may believe that the wrong person got a promotion, and you may even be right. If you are, the results of that decision will be revealed in due time. Keep your frustrations to yourself, and continue to do a great job. If the person who was promoted hangs himself through poor performance, you'll be looked to as the one who can save the day.

- **Being clueless about the big picture** and how your current position and your targeted promotion fit in with the company's goals and profitability picture. If you are serious about wanting a promotion, do your homework.

- **Being deceitful or double-minded** by acting in a respectful manner around your manager and then undermining or criticizing your manager in his absence. This *never* pays off!

- **Asking to be promoted without having gone above and beyond in your current position.** Employers don't promote someone for simply doing what's expected of them. You will not score any points with your boss by simply showing up and doing your job. You must make an effort to go beyond the requirements of your job description.

- **Expecting a promotion without having made measurable progress** in areas outlined for improvement on prior performance evaluations. If you haven't made any effort to improve on areas pointed out to you, why would your boss think you'd be a good study on a new job?

- **Being unprepared with talking points about the value or return-on-investment you'd bring in the new position.** Be clear about what you bring to the table and the strengths that are of value to the company.

- **Not dressing, speaking, or acting the part.** Don't stand out by being different. Stand out by being excellent. Dress in a manner similar to people two levels above you. If you wear something that causes your listener to pay more attention to it than your message, ditch it.

What to Expect

Getting promoted is not for the faint of heart. It takes a proactive plan, proof of performance, the right perception of you, perseverance, and a positive attitude. In the pages that follow, you'll learn what you might expect in each area.

Proactive Plan

The elements of a proactive plan include the following:

- Courageous conversations with your manager about your career and how you'd like to contribute to the company in the future.

> **Tip:** Be noticed for your excellence, not your lifestyle! One career coach shares the story of her 20-year-old daughter "Jane" who was into Goth a few years back. Jane was going to work with black nail polish, black lipstick, and gothic wraps around her wrists. She was adamant about "doing her thing" with the attitude that coworkers would just have to adjust to her. She lasted only a few months at the job. She's since shifted to standing out by being excellent.

- A winning combination of hard skills and soft skills. Hard skills include an up-to-date technical skill set and industry knowledge, whereas soft skills encompass your communication, presentation, and social skills.

- Strategies to overcome any challenges, such as being relatively new to the company, maneuvering through internal politics, patching up a tenuous relationship with your current manager, or any other of a number of challenges (see chapter 5 for tips on overcoming challenges).

- Mentors or "career champions" who will support you or be your accountability partners in the process.

Working with Coaches, Mentors, and a Personal Board of Advisors

One of the best ways to move your career forward faster is to work with a career coach. Coaching puts you and your agenda first, helping you gain self-awareness, set grander goals, create a more meaningful life, build momentum, and leverage multiple layers of learning for surprising success. For a list of certified career coaches, visit the following sites:

- www.CareerCoachAcademy.com

- www.LeadershipCoachAcademy.com

- www.CMInstitute.com

If you request someone to be your mentor, choose wisely. You'll want someone who

- Admires you (and whom you admire)!

- Will be completely objective.

- Has successful experience beyond the level of responsibility to which you aspire.

- Understands your industry, as well as the players and politics within your company.

- Does not see you as any kind of a "threat" to his career success.

- Can introduce you to important colleagues and his sphere of influence.

- Derives deep satisfaction from seeing you grow and succeed.

Your mentor(s) can be inside or outside your company. Avoid friends or family members—although they may have good intentions, they can't be as objective or knowledgeable about industry situations as you need at this juncture in your career.

A personal board of advisors takes the mentor concept a step further. Here, you gather a small group of individuals who have agreed to invest time in your career success. Depending on your needs and the availability of board members, meetings might be monthly or bimonthly, in person or by telephone conference. (Free telephone conferencing lines, called "bridge lines," are available at www.freeaudioconferencing.com and www.freeconferencecall.com).

When assembling your board, consider some of the items listed above for selecting mentors. In addition, ask people inside *and* outside your industry— the diversity will give you a wealth of perspectives and ideas.

Whether meeting with a mentor or your personal board of advisors, be prepared with

- Wins! Sharing successes creates momentum.

- Questions and an open mind on how to handle specific circumstances.

- Challenges you are facing, action you've already taken, and additional ideas you're considering.

- Insights (especially around situations that didn't work out as you hoped) to underscore your commitment to learning.

- A "give-back"—meaning something that will benefit the people who have made time in their busy schedules just for you. This could be as simple as sharing an inspirational quote or story, an interesting article that has application to all involved, a review of a popular new book, and so on.

- A well-trained replacement for the position opening you'll create when you get promoted. If you've been doing a great job in your current role, your manager may be hesitant to promote you because of the loss of productivity your absence will create.

- A calendar to schedule action steps and follow-up.

- A list of "controllables" that you can take charge of to keep momentum rolling.

- Research on comparable salary schedules.

The Value of a Mentor

"Elizabeth" had been employed with a large insurance organization for five years. During that time, she had applied to eight different promotional opportunities, and not once did she get a response. After enrolling in the organization's mentor program, Elizabeth asked her mentor for "political" wisdom on how to follow up on an application for which she had previously posted her resume. Elizabeth followed her mentor's advice on how to contact the hiring manager. After doing so, the hiring manager e-mailed Elizabeth within hours and wrote "We're so sorry we hadn't noticed your application earlier. You would have been perfect for the position, but we are in the middle of making an offer to someone else. We definitely would like to speak to you though for other opportunities."

Proposal and Proof of Performance

The elements of your proposal and proof of performance include the following:

- Your original job description, an updated version of your job description if you're doing more than when you started, and a proposed job description that captures the direction you'd like to take your position next.

- Documentation of your expanded skill set and track record since starting with the company (or in your current position).

- Proof of your coachability and openness to taking suggestions, constructive criticism, and direction.

- Your internal resume or summary of accomplishments relevant to the target position that captures bottom-line, return-on-investment contributions you've made to the organization.

Perception

When it comes to how your manager and others perceive you, you're on 24/7. Your brand image and behavior must be consistent and impeccable, no matter what you're doing or who's watching.

- Career Coach Kathy Bitschenauer of Washington-based New Pathways points to an article in CNNMoney.com's Business 2.0 magazine as a reminder of why you should never let down your guard. When candidates for a position with Southwest Airlines are flown to headquarters for an interview, they are given a special ticket. Unbeknownst to the candidate, this ticket alerts all staff—from ticket agents to aircraft crew—that this passenger is a job candidate. All along the way, the candidate is observed by Southwest employees who report to headquarters details about the candidate's behavior and demeanor. Any rudeness, lack of courtesy, or impolite behavior towards anyone, including passengers, spells disaster for the candidate. Even if they ace the interview, the company will not hire them.

- As the old saying goes, perception is reality. Your manager must perceive you as the confident leader or capable professional that you are. If you've been taken for granted or under-recognized by your current employer, you will need to conduct a full-scale branding effort (see the following worksheet for a crash course in branding).

- You must perceive yourself as the confident leader or capable professional that you are. You'll have difficulty convincing others that you're promotable if you don't believe it yourself. Act the part! And, when all else fails, fake it until you make it.

A CRASH COURSE IN BRANDING

Your brand is your unique promise of value. With a clear career brand, you will stand out and be known for something substantive and appealing that can't be easily replicated. That "something" will likely include a combination of subject-matter expertise and style. To help clarify your brand, ask yourself these questions:

What unique combination of professional skills or industry knowledge do people recognize in you?

_____

_____

What do people in the work world trust most about you?

_____

_____

What are you passionate about doing within the world of work?

_____

_____

What adjectives would those who know you well (your boss, coworkers, colleagues, friends, family members) use to describe you?

_____

_____

What reputation are you most proud of?

_____

_____

(continued)

(continued)

What products/services are you most passionate about?

_____

_____

What roles or titles do colleagues most associate you with?

_____

_____

If you could have just *one* impact on your work-world (your professional sphere of influence), what would it be?

_____

_____

What's your value proposition? For example, "I make money for my employer/clients by _____

_____

_____[fill in the blank]."

Using your answers from the preceding questions, write a draft of a brand statement below. Here's an example:

As a turnaround strategist, I draw from my management consulting experiences at a Big 4 firm and my Wharton Executive MBA degree with an emphasis in Ethics to take business ventures that have suffered at the hands of corrupt corporate executives and revitalize their people and profits.

_____

_____

_____

_____

_____

_____

Perseverance and Patience

Many factors can slow the process of your promotion. So you must practice patience and perseverance.

- Don't expect your manager to start a full-scale career-development initiative for you after just one conversation about your career aspirations. It's more likely that your manager will get wrapped up in all the other things he needs to do to manage, causing your promotion to be relegated to the back burner. Make it your responsibility to revisit the conversation, without being too pushy, at appropriate intervals.

- Often other pieces of the puzzle have to move into place before you can be promoted. For instance, the company may be waiting on a new customer to sign a contract, for budgets to be finalized, or for other people to be promoted. It's a chess game that, in addition to strategy, will take perseverance and patience.

Positive Attitude

Following are some key ways to exhibit a positive attitude:

- Waiting for your manager to respond to your promotion request can feel like a stress test. And, because your manager will evaluate your ability to manage stress when determining your promotion, look at this as an opportunity to shine.

- Ask yourself this future-focused question: "When I look back on this period of working toward my promotion, what kind of attitude will I want to have displayed?" Make sure it's an attitude you can be proud of a year from now.

Five A's to Your Game Plan

Like writing down goals, putting your action plans and a timetable on paper makes them concrete, increases your likelihood of achieving them, and helps you stay focused. Just as your DNA is unique, your game plan will be unique. Action steps appropriate to your situation will become more clear to you as you read each chapter and go through the process.

In general, everyone can count on going through the following five phases, each of which begins with the letter *A:*

- Act "as if."

- Angle from a "them" (not "me") perspective.

- Ask for what you need.

- Achieve and follow through with results

- Agree on a win-win arrangement

Act "As If"

The "Act" phase is the period prior to the promotion conversation where you act "as if" you were already in your new role (even though you may not have the title and benefits yet). This doesn't mean that you can assume authority beyond company policy. It does mean that you should demonstrate, ahead of time, that you can do the job and are doing it in many ways already. Employers love to see this because it takes the risk out of the promotion. They will be much more likely to promote you if they know you can, indeed, do the job!

Angle from a "Them" (Not "Me") Perspective

Strategize from a "them" (not "me") perspective. What will be most enticing to your employer? How can you best appeal to them? Identify opportunities or ongoing projects that align with your employer's global direction and goals—look for situations where things that need to be done aren't getting done. Come up with ideas and solutions that would make a bottom-line difference. Analyze where your manager needs the most help and how you could be of support. Gather input from your coach, mentors, and key people inside the organization. With the support of objective colleagues, consider possible changes to maximize your image, appearance, attitude, speech, or wardrobe. Determine what resources or tools you need for your promotion campaign, such as the following:

- A special report or research on a hot area for your company/industry

- A position proposal or job-description comparison itemizing the many additions you've made to your current job description

- A "one-sheet" that outlines the different ways in which you can contribute

- Your updated internal resume emphasizing your ROI (return on investment) achievements

- Your brand bio

- Your value statement

Ask for What You Need

Ever hear the saying, "you have not, because you ask not"? Don't assume that your manager will promote you just because you're doing a good job (although in some instances, it might happen this way). You must tell your manager what it is you want more of. You'll learn conversation starters and language techniques in chapter 4. It may seem counter-intuitive at first, but you'll see why *avoiding the word "promotion"* can get you ahead. In this phase, you'll query your manager on important issues, collaborate on possibilities, communicate the expectations you have for the desired outcome, and come away with a clearer picture of the action steps necessary to move ahead.

Achieve and Follow Through with Results

After the "Ask" phase, you'll need to follow through and deliver "home runs" on the action steps your manager requires. This can be a challenging time if the follow-through requires project work in addition to your current work, but it will be an opportunity for you to show how you can work smart and not just hard. This is often the hardest phase because it requires diligent, consistent follow-up. A positive and upbeat attitude is critical during this time, even if there are moments when it looks like you might not get what you want!

Agree on a Win-Win Arrangement

Make sure all your effort doesn't simply mean more work without the accompanying benefits you're after…benefits such as title, salary, perks, project ownership, and so on. In this phase, you'll negotiate on the expectations set up in the "Ask" phase and come to a win-win agreement.

Outline Your Timetable

Have you ever seen a "round tuit"? It's about the size of a quarter, made of wood, with the words "round tuit" written on both sides. It's shorthand for the best intentions of "I'm intending to get *around to it.*" This little coin is a tangible reminder to turn intention into action. There are several ways you can do just that.

Promotion Plan Timetable

Create a timetable system that works for you. Table 2.1 shows a Promotion Plan Timetable with example action steps.

Table 2.1: Sample Promotion Plan Timetable

Action Step	Resources/ Pre-Work	Follow-Up	Accomplish by Date	✓
Self-reflection on what I really want in my next career move and whether it's available with my current employer.	Journal. Write job description for my "dream job."	Talk with my spouse.	1st of this month	☐
Get input from others on how I can do better at acting "as if" I already have the promotion.	Review past performance evaluations and 360° feedback.	Get feedback from a few trusted colleagues to ensure I'm on target.	3rd of this month	☐
Meet with coach/ mentor as soon as possible to strategize the best angle for how/when to approach my manager.	Existing job description, list of accomplishments/ learning. Write out talking points to role-play conversation with mentor/coach.	Turn my rough notes into a polished one-page document. Ask Jane D. (a director in another department whom I trust completely) to	5th of this month	☐

© JIST Works

Action Step	Resources/ Pre-Work	Follow-Up	Accomplish by Date	✓
		review and give feedback on the documents, as well as my talking points. Work with coach on branding.		
Talk with two other management team members (Anne, Luis) to learn if there's any inside information I should know about before approaching my manager.	Review the projects Anne and Luis are working on to familiarize myself with them.	Be watching for an interesting factoid that would be helpful/of interest to Anne and Luis and e-mail as a "thank you" for their helpful information. Take some time and let all of the information gathered over the past few days marinate.	5th of this month	☐

(continued)

(continued)

Action Step	Resources/ Pre-Work	Follow-Up	Accomplish by Date	✓
Ask for conversation with manager about my commitment to make progress.	None.	Draft a before-and-after job description showing all the new things I've taken on in the past eight months.	8th of this month	☐
Brainstorm ideas with coach/mentor of how I can continue to grow my skills and contribute to the company, and identify specific information about how those contributions would benefit the company.	Company literature, annual reports, mission statement, talk with a department manager/VP and mentor.	Share my findings with my coach/ mentor.	9th of this month	☐

Action Step	Resources/ Pre-Work	Follow-Up	Accomplish by Date	✓
Meeting with manager. My agenda is to not let the conversation get sidetracked and be clear with him about my commitment to growing my career with this company; and to act confident so that he begins to change his perception of me and see me as the leader that I am.	Proposal information developed during meeting with mentor, as well as evaluations, before-after- and-beyond job description. (Note to self: I won't necessarily bring these out in the conversation, but it may be helpful to have them ready, depending on how the conversation goes.) Practice using benefit-oriented language so that manager sees the positives for company of promoting me.	Type up detailed notes from conversation while it's fresh in my head; create a timeline of accomplishments/ skill development I want to see happen between now and next month; calendar a date with my manager to revisit the discussion.	11th of this month	☐

(continued)

(continued)

Action Step	Resources/ Pre-Work	Follow-Up	Accomplish by Date	✓
Use assessments to better understand my strengths as well as any natural blind spots I need to be aware of.*	Assessments (online, check if HR department has anything available).	Work with coach to shore up any weaknesses.	17th of this month	☐
Focus on three items my manager indicated would be important for taking on more responsibility (take more initiative on finding solutions; work on my presentation skills; and see the big picture in my day-to-day work).	Add to my daily to-do lists a checkbox item called "see the big picture" to help me remember this. Read the book *How to Get Your Point Across in 30 Seconds or Less* by Milo Frank. Ask myself "what more can I do to solve this?" every time a new situation comes up.	Take time to review my progress at the end of each week on Friday afternoon.	19th of this month and weekly thereafter	☐

__Note:__ See appendix A for a chart of assessments and tools that can help jump-start the process of identifying your strengths and potential areas for development.

Action Step	Resources/ Pre-Work	Follow-Up	Accomplish by Date	✓
Pop my head into my manager's office to offer brief update on the progress I've made on his suggestions. Use the opportunity to discuss the new Ranier project and my idea about someone taking the lead on it.	Create MS Excel spreadsheet showing cost-benefit analysis of having someone (me, of course!) take a lead role on this project. Practice asking manager for a no-lose trial period.	To be determined after I meet with manager.	19th of this month	☐
Prepare a more formal proposal based on manager's nod last Friday to continue discussion with a few other managers.	Expand on my Excel spreadsheet, add more research, analyze how my new role will impact others in the organization (proves to my manager that I'm thinking "big picture").	Check with manager to make sure he's scheduled meeting with Sharon and Al. If not, ask him if I can do that for him.	23rd of this month	☐

(continued)

(continued)

Action Step	Resources/Pre-Work	Follow-Up	Accomplish by Date	✓
Meeting with manager, Sharon, and Al.	Think about what objections all three managers might have and think of options to overcome. Make sure I speak from a position of understanding the big picture and how this proposal benefits the organization (in addition to me!).	To be determined after meeting.	24th of this month	☐
One-on-one conversation with manager to nail down specifics on my new role and change in salary. Get very clear on his expectations so that I have clear marching orders.	Research salaries at salary.com to get a feel for averages in this geographic area. Practice delivering my value proposition.	Confirm that human resources received my manager's paperwork on this promotion! Get to work delivering beyond expectations!	25th of this month	☐

Your specific action steps may be different than this example. As things progress, you'll add items based on the outcome of conversations with your manager and others. Follow-up will be critical. Your manager may get busy with his day-to-day responsibilities. It will be up to you to stay upbeat about this and keep the ball rolling.

> **Note:** *See appendix A for chart of assessments and tools that can help jump-start the process of identifying your strengths and potential areas for development.*

A Simplified Version of the Promotion Plan

Another option is to create a simplified version of the Promotion Plan. Use legal-size paper or an MS Excel spreadsheet in landscape mode, as shown in table 2.2.

Table 2.2: Promotion Plan Timeline

Begin Date:	Date:	Date:	Date:	Date:	Date:	Date:	Target Date:
Action/ Progress	Action/ Progress	Action/ Progress	Action/ Progress	Action/ Progress	Action/ Progress	Action/ Progress	Final Outcome

As Stephen Covey advocates in his *7 Habits of Highly Effective People,* begin with the end in mind by filling in a description of your final outcome in the far-right column, such as "Account Supervisor role" or "Director position with influence on strategy and authority to impact bottom line."

If you want to incorporate your timeline into your existing PC or mobile calendar device, enter specific "meetings" that itemize what you plan to do and when you plan to do it.

The Storyboard Method

Finally, a third way to create a Promotion Plan with action steps is the storyboard method. The Walt Disney studio developed the concept back in the 1930s; today business uses this visual thinking process to help people brainstorm and generate consensus.

For purposes of planning your promotion strategy and timeline, and evaluating any gaps in your plan, a storyboard can help organize it all, like a flow chart. An easy way to make yours is to use large Post-It notes or index cards. Revisions to the plan are easy, as you can easily reposition, add to, or delete items as needed.

It doesn't matter which system you choose, as long as it's something that will keep you focused and moving forward. If you prefer the format in table 2.1, you'll find it repeated here with blanks for you to fill in.

Tip: *Harry I. Forsha, in his book* Show Me: The Complete Guide to Storyboarding and Problem Solving, *makes the case for using storyboards in business. According to Forsha, a storyboard consists of "a series of panels showing clearly, using pictures, numbers, and words, important changes, in order of occurrence, that taken together tell an interesting story." Storyboards are powerful because they engage the whole brain, both right- and left-brain functions. For information and examples of storyboarding, see www.apmp.org/ fv-156.aspx.*

Table 2.3: Promotion Plan Timetable Form

Action Step	Resources/ Pre-Work	Follow-Up	Accomplish by Date	✓
				☐
				☐
				☐
				☐
				☐
				☐
				☐

Key Points: Chapter 2

- Timing is everything. In 30 days, you can proactively prepare yourself for promotion. At the same time, there may be factors out of your control that will require patience on your part. If so, continue to deliver stellar results—this will only add to the evidence that you're worthy of promotion.

- In pursuing a promotion, avoid these common mistakes: focusing too much on you versus the company; going for too big a jump in responsibilities too soon; bugging your manager with too-frequent reminders of wanting to be promoted; begging for a promotion because of financial pressures; pouting, grousing, whining, or demanding; being clueless about the big picture; expecting a promotion without having made measurable progress; being unprepared with talking points about your bottom-line value; and not dressing, speaking, or acting the part.

- Earning a promotion is not for the faint of heart. It takes a proactive plan, proof of performance, the right perception of you, perseverance, and a positive attitude.

- Your proactive plan should include open, honest, and often courageous conversations with your manager about what you want and how you want to contribute; a winning combination of hard (technical) and soft (relational) skills; strategies to overcome any challenges or roadblocks; and mentors or "career champions" who will support you in the process.

- Proof of performance can be conveyed by providing an internal resume or summary of relevant accomplishments that captures your bottom-line contributions; a "before-after-and-beyond" job description that shows you're doing more than what is expected of you; and proof of your coachability and openness to taking suggestions and direction.

- Perception, or how others think of you, is critical. You won't get promoted to management if people think of you as a support person. Shift your manager's perception of you by first knowing how you want others to see you, and then living and breathing the part. And, get clear on your value proposition (for example, "I make money for my employer by _____ [fill in the blank]").

- Promotion is an endurance sport! This isn't a sprint you're in; it's a marathon. Perseverance and positive attitude will serve you well.

- Get a game plan. These five A's outline a powerful plan: Act "as if" you already had the new position; angle from a "them" (not "me") perspective; ask your employer for what you need (and also provide what they want); achieve and follow through with impressive, bottom-line results; agree on a win-win arrangement so that both you and your employer benefit.

- Outline a timetable and create a storyboard for yourself with specific action steps, deadlines, and follow-up appointments to create momentum and hold your vision for success!

Chapter 3

Your Promotability Factor

There are hundreds of factors that can affect your promotability! Remember the cotton story from chapter 2 and the many steps involved in producing a harvest? Well, there's another interesting piece to the story that has to do with the final yield.

Farmers want as much fiber as possible from each boll of cotton. An opened boll at harvest stage, which fits in the palm of your hand, contains four or five little dollops clustered together on a stem. Those dollops are officially called "locks." At harvest time, you can get either 4-lock or 5-lock cotton. Although the 5 lock variety is preferred, both types can be found on the same plant.

This variance made me curious. Expecting my favorite farmer to have all the answers, I asked, "And what does it take to get five locks instead of four?" I'd unknowingly asked the million-dollar question. The response was immediate laughter, followed by the declaration, "Pray!" I pressed on, "Seriously, Dad. Somebody must've done studies on this." He agreed, "Yes, there is research, but nothing conclusive. There are just too many variables."

As with growing anything, there will be dozens of variables that can affect the growth of your career. In this chapter you'll learn about the factors that will impact your success, not just with your current employer, but for a lifetime.

The 10 Commandments for Career Success

The factors that impact your career success can be boiled down to some critical truths, which I'll refer to lightly as the "10 Commandments" for career success:

Thou shalt

1. Manage thyself ... don't expect someone else to do it for you!

2. Know, and make known, your purpose, brand, and value.

3. Master your craft and increase your capacity to deliver results.

4. Walk in integrity, excellence, and optimism—at all times.

5. Lead, even if you're not in a formal leadership position.

6. Communicate articulately and persuasively.

7. Build a relationship with and respect your manager's authority, even when you don't think it's deserved.

8. Remember that it "takes a village" to raise a career, so build and nurture your work relationships.

9. Look and act the part.

10. Understand the big picture and the bottom line, and make regular contributions to both.

In the pages that follow, you'll see 150 suggestions for living by the preceding commandments. These were compiled from years of coaching career-minded clients, interviews with corporate managers, as well as experts in career development, coaching, leadership, organizational development, and management consulting. Special thanks go to Nancy Branton of PeoplePotentialGroup.com, Jane Cranston of ExecutiveCoachNY.com, New York City–based career coach Dale Kurow, and Dr. Ronald Page of www.HRConsultantsInc.com.

Some items in the list may seem obvious; some may be new; some may seem lofty. Consider sharing this list with your mentors to get their input on any additions or modifications they think are necessary for promotion within your organization. As you read through the lists, place a checkmark next to the items that are currently true for you.

1. Manage Thyself…and Don't Expect Someone Else to Do It for You!

❏ I am proactive about managing my career and do not expect others to do this for me.

❏ I have sketched out career goals for myself and am always open to considering new opportunities that align with the current vision and values I hold for my life and work.

Know Your Values!

In a 2005 article of the *Journal of Organizational Behavior,* Peter Heslin distinguishes between linear and nonlinear careers. Linear careers are focused on climbing the ladder within organizations to positions of greater authority. Nonlinear careers are characterized by a "lifelong commitment to developing a high level of skill in a particular field or specialty, periodic shifts between related occupational areas, specialties or disciplines, or regular changes between often seemingly unrelated careers."

He continues, "A commonality is often a deeply held commitment to discovering one's personal values, before shaping a career that satisfies these values."

To know what will be satisfying to you in your career, you must know your values!

❏ I sense that I am ready to stretch myself, accept additional responsibilities, learn new things, and take my career to the next level.

❏ I am clear on what I truly need in my next career move and believe it is possible to achieve that with my current employer.

❏ My motives for wanting a promotion are rooted in making a valuable contribution to my employer and are not based solely on making more money.

❏ I have sought out a mentor(s) who provides wise counsel about my career development, with discussion around how to improve my skills, avoid obstacles, overcome challenges, expedite the process, and relate to managers.

❏ Within my organization, there are individuals senior to me whom I might call my "career champions"; these people endorse me to management as a viable candidate for promotion—they go to bat for me with management (for example, "If we don't do something for this person, we'll lose her!").

❏ I have acted on the advice and counsel of my mentors and career champions.

❏ I manage my moods and don't allow emotions to dictate the quality of my day.

❏ I have a solid work-life balance.

❏ I work well with little direction; others perceive me as self-directed and self-managed.

❏ I have personally paid for my continuing professional development courses when necessary to acquire critical skills.

❏ In the event a promotion isn't possible with my current employer, I have a "Plan B" and am ready to market myself externally should I decide to move on.

❏ I am confident I'd bring value to other employers and know at what point I would leave my current employer.

2. Know, and Make Known, Your Purpose, Brand, and Value

❏ I know my purpose in life, and my career supports the fulfillment of that purpose.

❏ I have clarified a compelling career brand that conveys the subject-matter expertise I am passionate about, my unique style, and the value I bring to employers.

Flaunt Your Quirks!

Personal branding expert Kirsten Dixson, coauthor of *Career Distinction: Stand Out by Building Your Brand* (Wiley, 2007), maintains that standing out is about differentiating yourself. Dixson recommends, "Don't hide what makes you different. Accentuate it."

To get a good handle on your brand, consider a 360-degree instrument. Many employers use these to gather feedback and perceptions from managers and peers about an employee's performance. If your organization does not use this type of instrument, check with your manager for approval on conducting your own research on your personal brand attributes using a tool such as the 360Reach available at www.reachcc.com/360reach.

❏ I am able to articulate the bottom-line value I bring to my employer.

❏ My mentor would say that I have a balanced perspective on value: I believe I do not overestimate my value, nor do I underestimate it.

❏ I have logical and realistic beliefs around salary and am not embarrassed by or apologetic about the amount of money I make (or will make in my next position); I am confidential about my salary, and share this information only with those who need to know.

❑ When the topic of salary comes up with my manager, I focus on the value the company receives (or will be receiving) from my contributions (and not on what salary I need to make ends meet or on what someone else in the company received).

❑ I have researched salary trends for my profession; I have talked with network contacts in other companies about current salary rates for my target position. (See chapter 6 for more on salary research.)

❑ I have a written "career visibility" plan for getting on the radar screen of people who are important to my career success.

❑ I ask to sit in on meetings that people at my level might normally not attend as a way of becoming known and trusted.

❑ I know the key players and most influential people in my organization.

❑ The key players and most influential people in my organization know me.

❑ I know the key players and most influential people beyond my employer and within my industry.

❑ The key players and most influential people in my industry know me.

❑ I have carefully documented all of my contributions to my position, team, department, company, and/or customers, emphasizing the return-on-investment I bring to the company.

❑ I have been proactive about preparing for performance evaluations, carefully documenting the many contributions I have made, improvements in performance, additional tasks taken on, and new skills acquired over the last review period.

❑ I have saved "kudos" from my customers/clients, supervisor, and others within the organization as a way to help document my contributions.

❑ When team goals are achieved, I find ways to "celebrate" and honor everyone's contributions so that more than just our team (executives, other departments, other teams) are aware of the achievement.

❑ If I work late or on weekends to put in a special effort on a project, I occasionally make my manager aware of this in a tactful manner (for example, by sending my manager an e-mail during this time so that the time-stamp is on it).

❏ My manager views my overtime as "extra effort" and not an inability to get my work done in the normal amount of time.

❏ If my assignment is one that requires me to be out of the office regularly, I make an extra effort to be visible to, and communicate with, my manager.

3. Master Your Craft and Increase Your Capacity to Deliver Results

❏ I am passionate about my work and continually push myself to improve.

❏ I am coachable and open to trying new concepts or different ways of doing things.

❏ I have learned at least one new significant skill in the past year.

❏ I am ahead of the curve in some manner, whether in my skill set, communication abilities, industry knowledge, or emotional intelligence.

❏ My manager has outlined specific skills that I can work on to be considered for promotion, and I have been making measurable progress toward these skill levels.

❏ I volunteer for projects that expand the scope of my skills and knowledge.

❏ I am able to solve complex, work-related problems and figure out "workarounds"—alternative solutions to get things done when obstacles surface or others assume it can't be done.

❏ I am able to drive results by taking the next appropriate step that will bring tasks/projects closer to completion.

❏ I give priority to urgent and important matters and do not let urgent but less critical matters diminish my productivity.

❏ I tackle the tasks and issues that need attention and do not procrastinate.

❏ My intuition is an asset; situations where my "gut" has prompted me to act or speak up turned out better than they would have had I not.

❏ I respond promptly to e-mails and voice mails that have important subject matter.

❏ I am accessible to managers, team members, or other important people who rely on my input or participation for successful results.

❏ I double-check or proofread my work to maintain a consistent level of quality.

❏ I am persistent in following up at appropriate intervals, whether it be an hour, day, week, month, or year later; I have a "tickler" system for follow-up.

❏ I have an above-average level of technical skills relevant to my profession.

❏ I possess the level of industry knowledge and company insights needed for promotion.

❏ Others consider me to be of average or above-average intelligence.

❏ What I may lack in intelligence, I make up for in hard work and perseverance.

NY Times *Survey of Desired Skills*

Beta Research Corporation, on behalf of the *New York Times Job Market*, interviewed 250 hiring managers in the New York metropolitan area to learn which skills were most in demand. They said the following:

- Ability to work in a team environment (89 percent)
- Ability to learn quickly (84 percent)
- Presentation/verbal communications (76 percent)
- Multitasking (73 percent)
- Time management (69 percent)

Skills most in demand for management candidates were the following:

- Leadership (67 percent)
- Strategic thinking (56 percent)

Skills most in demand for administration candidates were the following:

- Technical (25 percent)
- Analytical (24 percent)

Skills most in demand for entry-level positions were the following:

- Ability to learn quickly (32 percent)

(continued)

(continued)

Further, employers said they were willing to pay more money to candidates with proficiency in the following:

- Multitasking (65 percent)
- Can quickly learn on the job (64 percent)
- Possess strategic-thinking abilities (61 percent)

4. Walk in Integrity, Excellence, and Optimism—At All Times

❏ I keep my word.

❏ My coworkers, customers, and managers trust me.

Joining Versus Leaving an Organization

TalentKeepers, a leader in employee-retention solutions, has done extensive research on what leads people to join, as well as leave, an organization. The top three reasons that people join an organization, in priority order, are the following:

- Organizational factors (pay, benefits, reputation)
- Job factors (duties, schedule, training)
- Leader factors (trustworthy, coach, flexible)

Interestingly, those priorities are flip-flopped when it comes to why people leave an organization. Cited as the number-one reason why people leave an organization was

- Leader factors

Your relationship with your manager might not seem important when signing on to an organization, but it's sure important for staying! Lack of trust with your leader/manager, the leader/manager's inability to coach and develop you, and the leader/manager's inflexibility about when to bend the rules and when not to are all important factors in good leadership.

The takeaway from this research is twofold:

1. When making a career move, go the extra mile in learning about how your manager manages. You may just decide it's a deal-breaker if your manager-to-be isn't trustworthy, doesn't operate from a coaching mentality, and won't be flexible.

2. As you move forward in your career, you will likely have opportunity to manage people (if you don't already). Your ability to retain those people will have much to do with your trustworthiness, ability to coach and develop others, and flexibility.

❏ If there is gray area on an ethical issue, I take the high road and do what is right.

❏ I do not take credit for ideas or work of others.

❏ I regularly put forth effort to do a great job, not just a good job.

❏ I have a good balance of confidence and humility.

❏ I can accept a compliment for a job well done and do not disagree with or ignore the compliment out of embarrassment or false humility.

❏ If I make a mistake, intentional or unintentional, I readily admit it and do not try to sweep it under the rug or share blame with someone else.

❏ If there is a difference of opinion, I do not insist that others agree with me, but intentionally try to understand their point of view.

❏ If any of my conversations were recorded and played back to others, I would not be embarrassed or ashamed by anything I have said about another person.

❏ I am known for delivering my projects or work on time or before deadlines.

❏ I am resilient and adapt to change quickly and positively.

❏ I easily adapt to other work roles assigned to me.

Tip: *To walk in integrity and excellence, consider this exercise. Bring to mind a person whom you admire and respect deeply. This may be someone you know or someone you don't know, such as a great business or political leader, philanthropist, or author. The person may be alive or passed on. Regardless, choose someone whose approval you would be proud to have. Now, pretend this person will see every product you create, every e-mail you write, and every word you speak. Would your "invisible boss" be proud of you and offer applause at the end of each day?*

❏ I have a mindset that sees the possibilities first and not the problems, opportunities and not obstacles, abundance and not barriers.

❑ Managers and coworkers would describe me as optimistic, generally happy, and pleasant to be around.

❑ Colleagues and others would describe me as having an above-average level of emotional intelligence and social skills.

❑ I think about how my actions will affect or be perceived by others, and not just about myself.

❑ I offer to help others when they need it, without compromising the quality of my individual productivity.

❑ I prepare for meetings by reviewing the agenda, thinking of solutions to issues, and having important information at my fingertips.

❑ When a manager or coworker asks me for information, I think about why the information is needed and offer additional resources that might be helpful.

Tip: *Leadership coach Nancy Branton of PeoplePotentialGroup. com suggests that, if you want others to trust that you're ready for a leadership role, get caught doing the job! For instance, when the executive team needs something done and your manager is on vacation, step up to the plate and take action. When various staff are working on different pieces of a project, take on the role of coordinating their activities. This way, when your managers are looking to add a leader, you're the natural choice.*

❑ I am careful to not "borrow" items from my employer that I have no intention of returning; I do not use employer time for personal activities.

5. Lead, Even if You're Not in a Formal Leadership Position

❑ I am comfortable and confident in expressing my opinions about work matters to my manager(s).

❑ When conflict arises, I address it professionally and do not overreact or avoid it.

❑ I take initiative on projects within my scope of authority and do not wait for someone to ask me to do something that I know I can/should do.

❑ I watch for and take informal opportunities to manage or mentor others.

❏ Coworkers perceive and look to me as a leader and motivator.

❏ Coworkers or those I currently supervise are growing professionally under my leadership.

❏ I speak up when appropriate in meetings where upper-level managers are present.

❏ I appreciate and acknowledge others' work and accomplishments.

❏ I am able to manage others to achieve both individual and organizational goals.

6. Communicate Articulately and Persuasively

❏ I consistently seek to enhance my communication skills, whether by reading, taking courses, participating in organizations such as Toastmasters, or acting on feedback from peers and mentor(s).

❏ Before speaking with my manager about opportunities for promotion, I rehearse with my mentor or coach to ensure that I sound professional, calm, and convincing.

❏ When making a business presentation, I am able to bring an attention-catching opening, structure, relevant data, stories of interest, and a clear summary to the material.

❏ I have been asked to lead team meetings or make presentations within my group/department.

❏ I have been asked to make presentations to key customers.

❏ When speaking, I am careful to enunciate so that people easily understand me.

❏ I have added at least three new words to my vocabulary in the past six months.

❏ I have a good command of English (or other primary language used in your business) and do not make grammar mistakes such as double negatives (for example, "It won't make no difference to her") or incorrect use of pronouns (for example, "Her and John went to the meeting").

❏ I avoid using profanity out of respect for others.

❏ When communicating by e-mail (internally or externally), I make an effort to be professional, recognizing that there will be a permanent record of everything I write.

❏ I have the technical skills to create a visually appealing PowerPoint presentation and know how to effectively integrate it into a business presentation (without relying on it so heavily that the point of the presentation is lost).

> **Tip:** *The blog Presentation Zen offers some helpful hints on PowerPoint: www. presentationzen.com/ presentationzen/. Check out the post, "What is good PowerPoint design?")*

The Timeless Trait

The past several decades have produced numerous studies that underscore the importance of communication skills.

- A 1998 survey conducted by the National Association of Colleges and Employers (NACE) indicated "good communication skills" as the top personal quality sought by employers evaluating a job candidate.

- Subscribers to the *Harvard Business Review* in a study by Bowman rated "the ability to communicate" the single most important factor in predicting the promotability of executives. In the study, communication skills were found to be more important than ambition, education, and capacity for hard work.

- A 20-year study of Stanford University MBAs found that the most successful graduates (as measured by career advancement and salary) shared the ability and desire to persuade, talk and work with others, and be outgoing.

- A survey of Fortune 500 vice presidents showed that 97.7 percent believed that "communication skills had effected their advancement to a top executive position."

7. Build a Relationship with Your Manager and Respect His or Her Authority, Even When You Don't Think It's Deserved

❏ I take the initiative to build a relationship with my manager, even when he/she is frustrating or difficult.

Abusive Bosses

Is your manager an occasional nuisance or a full-fledged bully? Any manager can have a bad day, but some completely cross the line into bullying and harassment. Wayne Hochwarter, associate professor of management at Florida State University's College of Business, studied employees with abusive bosses and found that:

- 31 percent of respondents reported that their supervisor gave them the "silent treatment" in the past year.

- 37 percent reported that their supervisor failed to give credit when due.

- 39 percent noted that their supervisor failed to keep promises.

- 27 percent noted that their supervisor made negative comments about them to other employees or managers.

- 24 percent reported that their supervisor invaded their privacy.

- 23 percent indicated that their supervisor blamed others to cover up mistakes or to minimize embarrassment.

For more information, see www.fsu.com/pages/2006/12/04/BigBadBoss.html.

Workers in the United Kingdom don't appear to fare any better, with Management-Issues.com reporting approximately 20 percent of all employees in the UK having experienced some sort of bullying or harassment over the past two years. (See www.management-issues.com/workplace-bullying.asp.)

If a bully boss is adding to your career pain, you'll find some camaraderie at www.hateboss.com, an online community just for venting your job frustrations!

❏ My manager and I have a relationship characterized by trust and respect.

❏ I "manage up" by communicating important information to my manager regularly, including regular status reports on major accomplishments, upcoming projects, and interesting happenings in the field.

❏ I understand my manager's goals and what deliverables are needed for him to be successful in his director's eyes.

❏ I understand the pressure that my manager is under.

❏ I have "career conversations" with my manager approximately every six months where I communicate my desire to grow in my skills and with the company. These conversations are separate and apart from my performance review.

❏ In career conversations with my manager, I emphasize language that conveys how I would like to "grow professionally" or "contribute to the company," as opposed to how I would like to "be promoted" or "get a raise."

❏ In career conversations with my manager, I ask specifically what it would take to get to my next career goal, obtain clear benchmarks, and obtain agreement from my manager that meeting those goals will result in promotion.

❏ I take constructive criticism from my manager and act on those suggestions to improve the way I do things.

❏ In team meetings, if a manager is wrong about something, I address it in a manner that does not embarrass or demean.

❏ In situations where my manager (or someone else) has been taking credit for my ideas or work (causing me to lose career momentum), I have changed my behavior to bring up new ideas in the presence of others, cc appropriate staff when communicating by e-mail, or add my name to reports that I have authored.

❏ I have no unresolved issues with my manager.

❏ I am viewed as the "heir apparent" for the position I am targeting (or to take my manager's place were he to be promoted).

❏ My manager has communicated to me in writing that I am being groomed for a promotion.

❏ I have taken my manager out to lunch in the last six months; the conversation centered on more than just business.

❏ The number of hours I work is similar to those of my manager or coworkers who are also being promoted.

❏ I have not been turned down for promotions in the past.

❏ I have not been passed over for promotion in favor of peers who have equal or less experience.

❏ If my manager has turned down a past request for promotion or salary increase, I have calendared another appointment and will work toward the skills that need improvement, and confidently return on the appropriate date with evidence of my accomplishments.

8. Remember That It "Takes a Village" to Raise a Career, So Build and Nurture Your Work Relationships

❑ I treat everyone respectfully, from coworkers to customers and janitors to senior execs, and not just the people whom I think can help me in my career.

❑ When communicating with my manager's boss, I do so with my manager's knowledge and permission so that my manager is kept in the loop.

❑ I speak respectfully about my manager, coworkers, and customers at all times, even if I think my comments won't get back to them.

> **Tip:** *Heed these words of wisdom from a senior manager who enjoyed an accelerated rise from field sales rep to senior district manager: "Always assume your coworker will be your boss the next day." You never know who may be given the reins of power!*

❑ My attitude toward others is consistent; I don't act differently when they are not around.

❑ I take initiative to build relationships with my manager's boss(es).

❑ I take initiative to build relationships with the company's executive team.

❑ I take initiative to build relationships with coworkers.

❑ I take initiative to build relationships with individuals from other departments within the organization.

❑ I take initiative to build relationships with customers/clients.

❑ I do not avoid developing relationships with people due to a lack of confidence or fear that I'm not important enough for their time.

❑ I have no unresolved issues with my manager's boss, coworkers, or customers.

❑ I have requested feedback from individuals in various areas/departments of the company in order to improve my performance.

❑ I have acted on this feedback to improve my performance.

❑ I have participated on cross-functional teams and performed well so that others outside my department are aware of my skills.

❏ I have held leadership roles on cross-functional teams.

❏ I am known for my ability to collaborate.

❏ I do not hesitate to reach out to others for their ideas, input, and expertise on matters.

❏ I operate within the confines of company policy; I don't "push the envelope," nor have I received warnings or reprimands.

9. Look and Act the Part

❏ My professional wardrobe is in fashion and in keeping with the expectations of my industry/company.

❏ I dress for success in a manner consistent with those in leadership at my employer.

❏ I do not dress more casually than my manager or manager's boss.

❏ My hairstyle or haircut has a contemporary look.

❏ (For women) I wear makeup, jewelry, and modest clothing that do not draw undue attention to me.

❏ I act professional, even when the boss is not around.

❏ When at social events or on business-related travel, I remain professional and avoid overindulging in alcohol.

❏ I do not spend excessive time at the "water cooler" (coffee station/ lunch room) if it means I will be associated with people who are not interested in developing their careers.

❏ I have an online presence; if you google my name, you'll find something positive!

10. Understand the Big Picture and the Bottom Line, and Make Regular Contributions to Both

❏ I currently work for a company that has experienced consistent annual growth in sales and profits.

❏ My values are aligned with my company's mission, and I focus on contributing to that mission in my work.

❏ I have a global perspective of the organization.

❑ I read the company's annual report and am familiar with its various marketing communication pieces such as the Web site, brochures, and sales material.

❑ I understand how my current position and my target position contribute value to the company's bottom line.

❑ My promotion target is a logical step up for me (as opposed to a giant leap over several levels of responsibility).

❑ I am currently performing some (or many) of the responsibilities of the position I want to be promoted to (perhaps without the title, salary, or formal authority).

❑ There is a succession plan in place for my current position; there is someone within the organization who is competent and well-trained to replace me.

❑ Without being asked, I take action within the bounds of my authority to leverage opportunities that will impact the profitability and productivity of my organization.

❑ I do not make suggestions without first considering how it would affect the entire team/department/organization.

Living Up to the 10 Commandments

How do you live up to all these commandments? One way is to be incredibly disciplined and committed. Another is to have work that is not simply a job, nor even a career, but truly a calling.

Is Your Position a Job, Career, or Calling?

Yale associate professor Amy Wrzesniewski, drawing on the influential work of Robert Bellah, studied the distinctions between job, career, and calling. The differences?

- In a **job,** the main goal of the individual is to bring home a paycheck; they do not seek many other rewards from their work.

- In a **career,** there is a deeper personal investment in work. Achievements are marked by income, social status, power, and prestige within their occupation.

- In a **calling,** fulfillment comes as a result of performing the work. Work is seen as an end in itself, rather than a means to income or advancement.

In which category does your current position fit best?

When your work is something you are passionate about, it will seem like a labor of love to bring your all to it. Recently, one of my friends was helping her daughter-in-law write a resume for a teaching position. I took a look at the rough draft and realized I could help make it better. I thought to myself, "I really don't have time to be doing this, especially with a publishing deadline looming," but I hated the thought of this wonderful teacher not putting her best foot forward. Passion makes a task lighter. And passion makes it purpose-driven. So make sure that passion is driving your promotion!

Calculating Your Promotability Factor

To get a sense of your promotability, count up all your checkmarked items from this chapter. Write your total here: _____

Although not an exact science, if you scored between

- 125–150: You are a high-potential performer on the fast-track to promotion.

- 100–124: You are on the right course for getting promoted.

- Fewer than 100: You have work to do, and that's what this book is all about!

LEVERAGING YOUR STRENGTHS AND DEVELOPMENT OPPORTUNITIES

Use the following space to identify your strengths, as well as opportunities for development, in each of the 10 areas.

1. **Manage thyself…and don't expect someone else to do it for you!**

What I'm already doing well in this area:

_____

What I will focus on improving and specific action steps I will take:

_____

_____

_____

---

2. Know, and make known, your purpose, brand, and value.

What I'm already doing well in this area:

_____

What I will focus on improving and specific action steps I will take:

_____

_____

_____

3. Master your craft and increase your capacity to deliver results.

What I'm already doing well in this area:

_____

What I will focus on improving and specific action steps I will take:

_____

_____

_____

4. Walk in integrity, excellence, and optimism—at all times.

What I'm already doing well in this area:

_____

What I will focus on improving and specific action steps I will take:

_____

_____

_____

5. Lead, even if you're not in a formal leadership position.

What I'm already doing well in this area:

_____

What I will focus on improving and specific action steps I will take:

_____

_____

(continued)

(continued)

6. Communicate articulately and persuasively.

What I'm already doing well in this area:

_____

What I will focus on improving and specific action steps I will take:

_____

_____

_____

7. Build a relationship with your manager and respect his or her authority, even when you don't think it's deserved.

What I'm already doing well in this area:

_____

What I will focus on improving and specific action steps I will take:

_____

_____

_____

8. Remember that it "takes a village" to raise a career, so build and nurture your work relationships.

What I'm already doing well in this area:

_____

What I will focus on improving and specific action steps I will take:

_____

_____

_____

9. Look and act the part.

What I'm already doing well in this area:

_____

_____

What I will focus on improving and specific action steps I will take:

_____

_____

_____

10. Understand the big picture and the bottom line, and make regular contributions to both.

What I'm already doing well in this area:

_____

What I will focus on improving and specific action steps I will take:

_____

_____

_____

Now that you've identified your strengths and crafted steps to shore up any weaknesses, read on to create a strategic plan for your promotion.

Key Points: Chapter 3

Although there are hundreds of factors that can affect your promotability, they can be condensed into some critical truths, referred to lightly here as the "10 Commandments" for career success:

1. Manage thyself—don't expect someone else to do it for you! Be proactive about your career. Live and work by the old saying, "If it's going to be, it's up to me."

2. Know, and make known, your purpose, brand, and value. Know yourself—what makes you tick, what drives you, what makes you passionate, what makes you of value—and then humbly campaign these virtues to those with the power to promote you.

3. Master your craft and increase your capacity to deliver results. Be passionate about your work and continually push yourself to improve.

4. Walk in integrity, excellence, and optimism—at all times. Trust is a more powerful asset than talent, skill, or impressive degrees.

5. Lead, even if you're not in a formal leadership position. Find your voice and let it be heard—professionally, confidently, and respectfully. Everyone is a leader.

6. Communicate articulately and persuasively. Master your ability to communicate. These skills can be enhanced through reading, taking courses, listening to audio training, or participating in programs such as Toastmasters. Don't think you'll get better without feedback—work with someone you trust to coach you and give you feedback so that you can measure your progress.

7. Build a relationship with and respect your manager's authority, even when you don't think it's deserved. Start by understanding what your manager needs and the pressure she faces. Take the initiative to "manage up" by communicating important information. As much as it is in your power, be responsible for making this relationship work.

8. Remember that it "takes a village" to raise a career, so build and nurture your work relationships. Treat everyone respectfully, from coworkers to customers and janitors to senior execs, not just the people you think can help you in your career.

9. Look and act the part. Your work attire should match that of your manager or your manager's manager. Act professional, even when the boss is not around!

10. Understand the big picture and the bottom line, and make regular contributions to both. Get a global perspective on your organization, including how you and your department fit in and how you can tangibly contribute to its most important goals.

Chapter 4

Crucial Career Conversations: T.A.L.K. It Out

Merriam-Webster's Online Dictionary defines conversation as

oral exchange of sentiments, observations, opinions, or ideas

Crucial conversations require straightforward and detailed delivery of ideas and information. This snippet of dialogue from a young newlywed couple reminds us that, without direct communication, conversations and relationships can "head south" pretty quickly!

Husband (clueless): What's up?

Wife (aloof, giving him the silent treatment): Nothing.

Husband (baffled): Are you angry with me?

Wife (frustrated): Well, what do you think!

Husband (confused but patient): I can't read your mind.

Wife (angry): Why can't you just figure out what's important to me!

Husband (losing patience): Then why can't you just tell me what's wrong?

Wife (hurt): Because if you really cared about me you'd figure it out just by paying attention!

Husband (lost patience): I give up!

Wife (exasperated): Fine!

Fortunately, a conversation like this would be rare in the corporate world, but it serves as a reminder that you must be clear and direct with your manager or your career may take a wrong turn. Don't make the mistake of expecting your employer to read your mind or know your career aspirations.

In this chapter we'll look at the crucial conversations that need to take place with your manager. As you think about your conversation, remember to T.A.L.K., which stands for

- **T = Timing:** When would be the optimal time to start the conversation with your manager?

- **A = Agenda:** What are the most important items to discuss?

- **L = Language:** What words will be most impressive?

- **K = Keep It Going!:** How will you keep the door open to return to this discussion in the weeks to come?

You'll see each of these items and more in the following sections. Before you review them, recognize that every situation will go a little differently, depending on

- Your manager's perception of you.

- The number of people who might be involved in authorizing a promotion.

- The history and current events within your organization.

- Your past record with the organization.

- And more!

With this in mind, make a commitment to discussing new insights or information and strategizing new action steps on a frequent basis (preferably with your coach or mentor). The one thing that is certain is that there will be twists and turns as the process unfolds.

Timing: A Time for Every Season

The wisdom of Solomon reminds us there is a time for every season. As chapter 2 explained, you can't expect to reap your harvest before you've planted seeds. Your career conversation will go more smoothly when you have

- Established a relationship of trust with your manager and others of influence.

- Performed beyond what your original job description calls for.

- Demonstrated an understanding of the global needs of the organization and how your role contributes to its profitability.

- Made noticeable progress on the skill sets your manager has recommended for development.

- Are known by and have visibility with other management members who can influence the promotion decision.

- Been with the company long enough that they recognize your potential and positive attitude.

When it's time for you to be proactive about your promotion, there will be two steps to the conversation:

- The first is to request a meeting—ask for one-on-one face-time with your manager.

- The second is the actual "career conversation"—the time when you discuss how your career progression will align with the company's goals.

Don't plunge into either without having done some information gathering and strategic planning.

Conduct Reconnaissance

Reconnaissance is the act of gathering preliminary information to determine your strategy. Your mission will be more successful if you first have some "reconnaissance" conversations with individuals "in the know."

Who might that be? In gathering information, start with other leaders who have regular contact with your manager. However, don't rule out someone who has a lesser role but has your manager's ear. It's not necessary to share with these people your end goal. Casual, nonchalant conversation should be the order of the day.

Decide how many people to speak with based on the size of your organization:

- If it's a larger company with multiple layers of management, speak to two or three others.

- If it's a smaller organization, a conversation with one person may suffice.

- For very small organizations (perhaps it's just you and your manager), reconnaissance conversations may not be appropriate. In this case, you'll need to do critical thinking on your own or with your coach or external mentor.

What do you ask during reconnaissance? In general, watch for any information that might give you leverage, such as

- Budget cutbacks or increases, or other changes in allocation of resources

- Changes in staffing

- The next career move your manager wants to make

- Any plans for growth or new projects that will require extra manpower

- Situations where your manager or others are overloaded and not getting work done that impacts the bottom line

> **Tip:** *Contrary to popular opinion, you don't have to wait for a performance review to start the promotion conversation, nor do you need to frame the conversation around your career. Linking it to a new project, a change in operations, a new client, or a change in management will give the appearance that you are very team oriented.*

In addition, ask questions that will help you gain a global understanding of what's happening in the company and the pressures your manager faces. For starters,

> What do you see as the company's key priorities for the next 6 to 12 months? Where do you think my manager could use the most support to allow him to be more effective?

Of course, if the answers to these questions are information you should be intimately familiar with already, bump up your questioning to demonstrate a greater degree of understanding. For example,

> I understand the Walker project is close to getting funding. As we look at the resources needed to support that, I'm concerned that the scalability of our current IT system won't accommodate it. What are your thoughts?

Assembling reconnaissance data allows you to identify the symbiotic relationship between your career and the company's needs, which makes a win-win for everyone.

Request a Meeting

When it comes to asking your manager for a meeting, avoid times when a big deadline is looming, an internal crisis has just occurred, or a reduction in force is happening.

Even the day and time you approach your manager should be considered. Monday mornings are often hectic, so opt for another day. If your boss has one or two days during the week that are normally heavier than others, avoid those days as well.

In requesting a meeting, frame it in the context of a benefit to the company. For instance:

Before:

"I'd like to talk to you about my career today."

After:

Kudos on the Walker project!

[Your manager thanks you for the compliment, and then you follow with]

I had some ideas on how the company could better service that contract.

[Your manager's ears perk up; she wants to hear more.]

Do you have some time on your calendar in the next few days, or, better yet, how about lunch sometime this week?

> **Tip:** *How does your manager like to be approached when it comes to hearing new ideas? If he is more introverted than extroverted, he probably won't like being surprised, so give a hint as to what the conversation will be about when making the request. If you're dealing with an extrovert, he may be fine with an impromptu meeting. Extroverts often think by talking and enjoy exploring ideas through extended conversation.*

The "Before" language has more potential to put the manager into a mode of defensiveness, possibly thinking to herself, "What do you mean, 'your career'! We've given you tons of opportunities already at this company. Are you ungrateful? Am I going to have to come up with some solution for this?"

The "After" language piggybacks the conversation on the company's priorities. Now, it appears that you are the one *offering solutions.*

The "request" might play out in any number of scenarios. If your manager is frequently interrupted at the office and having lunch together is not uncommon for the two of you, consider the lunch approach:

How's your calendar for lunch one day this week? I have some ideas I'd like to run by you.

If an office meeting is more appropriate, ask

What does your schedule look like in the coming week? I need 5 to 10 minutes of your time to get your insights on some goals I've outlined.

Of course, your manager may say, "I've got time; let's do it now!" so be ready with your agenda. (See "Agenda: Stick to a Plan," later in this chapter.)

Responding to a Posted Opening

There will be times when you won't have to go to the extra work of proposing a promotion to your manager. When there is an open position, the company will likely interview internal (and possibly external) candidates for the role. Just because your managers know you, don't skip any steps in approaching the interview process, including submitting your online application and preparing for interviews. This is a great opportunity to

- Freshen your brand so that people perceive you in the manner that's consistent with what you want.

- Update your resume with recent accomplishments and contributions, and create a compelling letter to accompany it.

- Practice articulating the insight you have into the company's needs and priorities, as well as the value you bring to the table.

- Submit materials that document that you have already been doing some (or all) of the responsibilities, or have the transferable skills to do so.

- Highlight what you see as the key deliverables for the position (based on your research) and prepare a business plan or action strategies you might use in your approach to the situation.

For a successful interview, be ready with an abundance of "SMART Stories™." A SMART Story™ will allow you to craft your interview responses with a definitive beginning, a meaty middle, and dynamite ending. This approach also is unique in that the final step positions you to neatly link the response back to your manager's question and focus the conversation on how you can do the job instead of simply auditioning for the job. Here's how a SMART Story™ breaks out:

- **Situation and More:** Frame the story with contextual details, offering specific numbers about the situation. What was the specific situation you were faced with? Use numbers to describe who and what was involved. Where and when did it occur? What was the impact of the situation? What was the timeframe of the story?

- **Action:** What specific action did you take to tackle the task, overcome the challenge, or resolve the issue? If others were closely involved, how did you interact with them? What were your thoughts or decision-making process? What was your specific role in relation to the team?

- **Results:** Essential to your success story are numbers-oriented, bottom-line results. They will help you convey your return-on-investment (ROI) value and give you leverage in salary negotiations.

  - What measurable outcome did you achieve? Think beyond your own work role to how others were impacted, including your boss, your team, your department, your company, your customers, your community, or your industry.

  - If it was a group effort, what measurable outcome did the group achieve or contribute to? Did you contribute to a 5 percent increase in productivity; support a team that met or exceeded goals by 9 percent in a difficult economy; participate in an effort that improved customer satisfaction scores; collaborate with team members to accomplish work with 25 percent less staff; or provide ideas that halted a conflict or impasse that had held up progress?

  - If the outcome wasn't rosy, what conclusions did you reach or what positives did you learn from the experience?

  - Compare your performance. You can make comparisons to a variety of numbers, including your prior work performance, the company's past record, the industry standard, or your competitor's average.

- **Tie-in and Theme:** Use a question or statement to link this story back to important issues or link it to a theme of key competencies your manager seeks. Statements might convey your enthusiasm or knowledge you've gained:

  - "I found that I thrived in these sorts of situations, as they give me a chance to use my problem-solving skills," or

  - "I learned that it's important to regularly communicate progress status to every member of the team," or

  - "From a recent conversation I had with one of our vendors, I know these strengths in vendor relations would be of help."

Note the numerous facts and figures included in this sample SMART Story™.

	SMART Story™
Situation and More:	*My role:* Office Manager
	Where: Inco Insurance (current employer)
	When/Timeframe: March through September of this year
	Who else was involved or impacted: Employees (25 claims processors and 5 support staff)
	What was the task or challenge: My challenge was to stop losses of more than $1,000 per month. I didn't realize that the systems I put in place would not only stop those losses but also increase our productivity. Here's what happened…
Action:	*What was your thought process? What steps did you take? What decisions were made? Describe the sequence.* As you know, I was new to the position and familiarizing myself with expenses. I compared and analyzed office expense figures with several prior years and realized that, even though our headcount was down by 25 percent, our expenses were up by almost 30 percent. None of our vendors had implemented any price increases, so I began to look for other reasons. I noticed that CDs and boxes of file folders seemed to be "walking off by themselves." In one of our weekly group meetings—something new I implemented to improve teamwork—I explained that one of our goals included cost controls. To help meet that goal, a new check-out system would be implemented for items valued in excess of $20, but that incidentals would be on an "honor system." I posted a bar graph in the supply room reflecting volume in use of supplies over the past six months, along with reduction goals for each ensuing month. I asked staff members for suggestions on incentives and decided what would be feasible. When we reached our monthly goals, I

	rewarded staff with their choice of an early-dismissal day or a catered box-lunch party. In fact, you [Mr. Manager] stopped by for one of our first celebrations!
Results:	Use numbers to relate your results. Supply costs were not only reduced more than 35 percent, there was greater camaraderie among the team. It has led to the claims processors openly sharing helpful resources and making suggestions, some of which were implemented and helped improve our productivity numbers by about 15 percent.
Tie-in/Theme:	It confirmed to me that communicating clear objectives to staff, along with soliciting their input, is a wise management policy.
Competency Theme:	Communications, problem solving, analytical, motivator

SMART Story™ Worksheet

To help identify accomplishments for your interview (and for your Competency & Contributions document that you'll learn about later in this chapter), use this SMART Story™ worksheet. (You can use the form in appendix B to make additional copies if needed.)

Situation and More:

Your role: _____

_____

_____

When: _____

_____

Who else was involved or impacted: _____

_____

(continued)

(continued)

What was the task or challenge? _____

_____

_____

_____

Action:

What was your thought process? What steps did you take? What decisions were made? Describe the sequence.

_____

_____

_____

_____

_____

Results:

Use numbers to relate your results.

_____

_____

_____

Tie-in/Theme:

Competencies:

_____

How this story ties to your organization's priorities and goals:

_____

_____

_____

_____

For a thorough review of preparing for the interview process, see *Interview Magic* (JIST Publishing). Now, on to the second step in the T.A.L.K. It Out process—your agenda!

Agenda: Stick to a Plan

Someone once said that for every minute spent in organizing, an hour is earned. Organize your thoughts before you broach the subject with your manager.

To formulate an agenda, you'll need to

- Know what you want.
- Know what your employer wants.
- Know what your manager wants.
- Know your value.
- Adapt your presentation to your listener.
- Offer supporting documentation.
- Briefly touch on salary, just so that your manager is aware that you're not volunteering to take on major new responsibilities without an increase in compensation (see chapter 6 for more on salary negotiations).
- Identify potential next steps.

Know What You Want

Go into the meeting knowing your objective. You likely want more of something, such as greater authority, responsibility, salary, and so on.

MY PERSONAL OBJECTIVE FOR THE CAREER CONVERSATION

Use this worksheet to clarify your personal objective for the upcoming career conversation with your manager. You may also find it helpful to review the "Promotion Goal" worksheet in chapter 1.

In my next career move, I want:

(continued)

(continued)

More authority? ___Yes ___No

How much? _____

_____

More responsibility? ___Yes ___No

What specifically? _____

_____

More strategic input? ___Yes ___No

On what issues?_____

_____

_____

A different project or team assignment? ___Yes ___No

If so, which one? _____

_____

A new title? ___Yes ___No

If so, what? _____

_____

More money? ___Yes ___No

If so, how much? _____

_____

Other ___Yes ___No

If other, describe: _____

_____

_____

Know What Your Employer Wants

Throughout this book you've seen the emphasis on making this conversation a win-win so that both you and your organization benefit. You've

just identified what you want. Now take a moment to clarify what the employer wants.

First, make sure you're meeting the competencies the employer has outlined for the position. Ask your manager or human resources department about these. Later in this chapter, you'll learn about creating a document that identifies specific accomplishments you've contributed relevant to each competency. Next, find something to fix!

YOUR EMPLOYER'S OBJECTIVE

Use this worksheet to clarify what you think your employer wants. Doing so will help you align your career advancement strategy with your employer's priorities.

Competencies outlined by my employer for my target position include _____

_____

_____

My employer's primary goals/priorities for my department/team in the near-term and long-term are _____

_____

_____

With respect to those goals, specific problem areas to address or processes to enhance include _____

_____

_____

I have already been focusing on these priorities in my current role by doing the following: _____

_____

_____

(continued)

(continued)

The specific, bottom-line results I have contributed to those
priorities include _____

_____

_____

In a promoted role, I would be able to make additional contributions
by doing the following: _____

_____

_____

The specific, bottom-line results I estimate I would contribute in this
new role are _____

_____

_____

_____

Know What Your Manager Wants

Your employer's wants and your manager's wants may, or may not, be the
same depending on the hierarchy of your organization. In situations where
your manager is also the business owner, the manager's and business' wants
will be identical. A level of complexity is added when there are multiple
layers of management. In this case, you must understand not only what
your manager wants, but also what your manager's supervisors want.

YOUR MANAGER'S OBJECTIVE

Use this worksheet to clarify whether your manager and employer are
after the same goals.

[If different from your employer's goals/priorities] My manager's primary goals/priorities for my department/team in the near-term and
long-term are _____

_____

From conversations with others and through observation, it appears my manager could use help with the following: _____

_____

_____

In a promoted role, I would be able to help my manager by doing the following: _____

_____

_____

_____

Know Your Value

There is no one-size-fits-all strategy for approaching your employer for promotion, except to make your case by providing value and an ROI. ROI (return on investment) is a business term widely used by companies to determine how quickly their decision to invest in new equipment, advertising, or an expansion will pay for itself. In the case of an employee, the employer is investing in salary, benefits, training, work space, and equipment.

Earlier in the chapter, you learned the importance of being direct and not assuming that the employer knows your career aspirations. That does not mean you need to lead off the conversation with what you want. Instead, starting off with what the other person wants is a more savvy strategy.

10 Ways to Create an ROI

You may be wondering how your position contributes a return on investment to your employer. It's easy to see when you're in sales, as your job is item #1—generate sales. Even if you're not on the sales front line, you can still impact the bottom line, as shown in items 2 through 9 here.

1. Generate income.
2. Cut costs.
3. Save time.
4. Make work easier.

(continued)

(continued)

5. Solve a specific problem.
6. Be more competitive.
7. Build relationships/an image.
8. Expand business.
9. Attract new customers.
10. Retain existing customers.

What the other person (your manager or company executives) typically wants is a profitable ROI. Smart career professionals concentrate on generating ROI for their employers. For instance, a top sales performer can show that a $125,000 salary will be justified by her ability to bring in $500,000 in new sales contracts. A materials manager might find methods to reduce waste or recycle scrap, which may add up to a six-figure savings. A production-line worker might make a suggestion that, when implemented, leads to a spike in productivity, which can be tied to the bottom line. Whatever you want in this promotion, challenge yourself to look for ways to boost your employer's success. Include both your prior contributions, as well as future projections, in your career conversation, as they will give you leverage in future salary negotiations.

This example describes a purchasing manager's ROI statement:

> I noticed that there were some holes in the system I inherited when it came to purchasing raw materials. By taking a "deep dive" in looking at that, changes were made that reduced our costs on raw materials more than 35 percent this past quarter, nearly a $60,000 savings. That number will probably be closer to a $90,000 savings for the upcoming quarter, which is typically our busiest. By year's end, we should be looking at a savings of $200,000+.

Tip: *Lauren, in her early 40s, wanted a director role within her organization. Although her immediate manager, a senior director, was the person with whom Lauren would start her career conversations, Lauren realized she would also have to gain the approval of the other directors and VP for her move. In the past, Lauren had been happy with being more or less "invisible" to upper management. Lauren needed a more concerted radar-screen campaign. She began by changing her traffic patterns so as to run into directors on a more regular basis. And she began speaking up with confidence in department meetings. Her strategies worked, in that other directors began to stop and ask Lauren her opinion on matters during casual encounters in the hallway.*

Here's an ROI example that a project manager created as a part of her promotion proposal to become a manager:

> With me focusing on this task, accuracy can improve a minimum of 2 percent per unit, or a $15,000+ savings. Looking at our inventory of 12,000 units, that translates to a potential $180 million savings to the company in the first year alone.

Note the languaging. The individual does not say "If you have me focusing on this task…" or "With someone focusing on this task" but inserts ownership of her idea by saying "With me focusing on this task…." We take a deeper look at the all-important languaging of your request later in this chapter.

MY RETURN ON INVESTMENT SOLUTION

To develop ideas that document the return on investment you've made to your employer, consider these questions:

- Where have you gone above-and-beyond to set yourself apart from your coworkers?

  _____

  _____

  _____

- Review prior performance evaluations for ideas or information that document your contributions. Write highlights of that material here:

  _____

  _____

  _____

  _____

- To help students learn, teachers use "realia"—objects that relate classroom teaching to real life. What realia would help your manager see the substance of your contributions? These might be reports written, brochures designed, products developed, Web site material created, letters of appreciation from customers, and so on.

  _____

  _____

(continued)

(continued)

- What measurable outcomes have been achieved as a result of your work? Think beyond your own work role to how others were impacted, including your manager, your team, your department, your company, your customers, your community, or your industry.

  _____

  _____

  _____

- If it was a group effort, what measurable outcome did the group achieve? Did it contribute to a 5 percent increase in productivity; support a team that met or exceeded goals by 9 percent in a difficult economy; participate in an effort that improved customer satisfaction scores; collaborate with team members to accomplish work with 25 percent less staff; or provide ideas that halted a conflict or impasse that had held up progress?

  _____

  _____

  _____

- Compare your performance. You can make comparisons to a variety of numbers, including your prior work performance, the company's past record, the industry standard, or your competitor's average.

  _____

  _____

  _____

Recall that in a prior worksheet, "Your Employer's Objective," you identified your future return on investment. If you did not answer that question previously, it's critical that you identify it here. ***Without it, you have a weak business case for promotion.*** For convenience, the item is repeated here.

The specific, bottom-line results I estimate I would contribute in this new role are _____

_____

_____

© *JIST Works*

Adapt Your Presentation to Your Listener

In addition to emphasizing the ROI, consider your manager's preference for taking in information and making decisions. Clues to this can be found in temperament and personality models established by David Keirsey, Ph.D. (creator of the Keirsey Temperament Sorter) and the mother-daughter team of Katharine Briggs and Isabelle Myers (authors of the Myers-Briggs Type Indicator, widely used in corporate America).

The basic tenets of personality type measure four scales:

1. **Energy:** The direction in which your energies typically flow—outward, toward objects and people in the environment (Extroversion, or its abbreviation E) or inward, drawing attention from the outward environment toward inner experience and reflection (Introversion, or its abbreviation I).

   What this means to your promotion conversations: First, be aware of your own preference and whether it is the same as or different from your manager's. If your manager has a preference for Extroversion, he may tend to be more verbal and prefer to think by talking.

   Introverts tend to be more pensive, so give them a heads-up about what the conversation involves, as well as time after the conversation to let ideas marinate.

2. **Perception:** Whether you prefer to take in information through your five senses in a concrete fashion, focusing on "what is" (Sensing, or S) or with a "sixth sense" in an abstract or conceptual manner, focusing on "what could be" (iNtuiting, or N).

> **Tip:** *Personality type influences promotion. For instance, the* MBTI Manual *(Third Edition, Consulting Psychologists Press) indicates that, on a national basis, only a small percentage of the population has the NT (iNtuiting-Thinking) combination (10.3 percent). Yet when comparing this percentage of the population with a sample of MBA students, the percentage of students reporting an NT preference was almost double that of any other type.*
>
> *Often, MBA graduate programs lead to an executive track, with opportunities for problem-solving, brainstorming, strategy, and leadership. This is perpetuated both from the standpoint of good job fit and the tendency for people to hire people similar to them (NT-type board members hiring NT-type executives).*

What this means to your promotion conversations: You can often spot people who have a preference for Sensing—they like to take in new information in a sequential, concrete, and ordered fashion. If this is your manager, provide information with numbered lists and sufficient detail.

Those with a preference for iNtuiting, however, like to hear the "big picture" first. When speaking to an individual with this preference, emphasize the strategic benefit to the organization and bullet-point key information only. Again, be aware of your own preference and how it may differ from your manager's.

> **Tip:** *Determine the essence of your personality with a free online personality instrument available at www.advisorteam.com. With an upgrade, you can access a full report that will help you understand your preferences and how they can improve your communications.*

3. **Decision-Making:** Whether you make decisions based on facts and logic (Thinking, or T) or based on personal or social values (Feeling, or F).

    What this means to your promotion conversations: Is your manager the detached, bottom-line type? If so, chances are good your manager has a preference for Thinking when it comes to making decisions. Make a strong business case with bottom-line data.

    If your manager has a preference for Feeling, use strong bottom-line data as well, but also emphasize the ethical benefit to employee morale and customer relations. Identify whether your own preference is the same as or different from your manager.

4. **Orientation:** Whether you orient your outer world in a methodical, deliberate manner, seeking closure (Judging, or J), or in a spontaneous, play-it-by-ear approach, remaining open to more information (Perceiving, or P).

    What this means to your promotion conversations: If your manager leans toward Judging, he will likely want to make a decision quickly. If Perceiving, he may want you to gather more information for consideration. Again, be aware of how your own preference may differ from your manager's.

In appendix C, you'll find a self-scoring personality instrument that you can use to gauge your own preferences in the four areas of Energy, Perception, Decision-Making, and Orientation of your environment. After scoring yourself, repeat the exercise and answer how you think your manager would respond.

Beyond personality preferences, you can also adapt your presentation to your manager's learning style, whether auditory, visual, or kinesthetic/tactile. Table 4.1 helps you identify and adapt to your manager's learning preference.

Table 4.1: How to Connect with the Three Learning Styles

Activity	Auditory Learning Style	Visual Learning Style	Kinesthetic/Tactile Learning Style
Words and phrases used	Uses words such as *hear*, *tuned in*, and *think* or phrases such as *sounds good*, *I hear what you're saying*, or *let me hear your explanation of that*.	Uses words such as *see*, *picture*, and *imagine*, or phrases such as *it looks to me as though*, or *let me get a clearer picture of that*, or *can you shed some more light on that subject for me?*	Uses words such as *feel*, *gut feeling*, and *comfortable*, and phrases such as *something doesn't feel right*, *feels good*, or *there is/isn't a connection there.*
Language	Likes to hear factual, sequential thought processes, with steps outlined in a logical linear fashion.	Likes to hear descriptive language to help create a picture in their mind.	Likes language that is conceptual or abstract; likes hearing metaphors; may describe knowing something to be true in their "bones" without being able to explain it logically to others.

When taking in new information at work	Prefers verbal instructions or talking about it with a colleague—needs to hear it to know it.	Prefers seeing demonstrations, diagrams, or pictures; likes things in view, with items color-coded—needs to see it to know it.	Prefers a hands-on, learn-as-you-do process—needs to do it to know it.
Translation of thoughts	Will pick up a thought and hear it as a word.	Will pick up a thought and see it as a picture.	Will pick up a thought and feel it as a sensation or associate it with some other memory.
Preference for business meetings	Can get just as much out of a telephone meeting as a face-to-face meeting.	Prefers face-to-face meetings.	Prefers meetings that involve an activity; provide something to engage in physically, whether a report they can hold or a sample they can touch.
Distractions	Stays focused on conversation and is not easily distracted by other activity in the room.	Notices other activity in the room.	Is easily distracted by activity around the room.
Note-taking behavior	May take minimal or no notes.	Takes notes; often doodles on the page.	Takes copious notes.

What Is Your Body Language Saying?

How you walk, stand, sit, and use body language all add to the overall impression you make. Pay attention to these items:

- **Walk:** Walk into a room as you if belong there—confident and alert. (Women, heed the advice of film stars for making an entrance—enter a room with your hips first. Doing so improves your posture and carriage.) As is the custom for royalty or important political figures (we know your manager isn't, of course), avoid exiting a room with your back to people. If possible, walk to the door with your manager; or, turn toward him as you head for the door and say something like, "I'll be sure to get you that follow-up information by Friday."

- **Stand:** Shoulders square, chest out, stomach held in, head held high. My high school marching band instructor used to holler during practice: "skyhooks in your ears...skyhooks in your ears"—a somewhat uncomfortable reminder to stand tall, with heads held high!

- **Sit:** Men, no crossed legs or slouching in the chair. Women, sit like royalty—spine straight and legs crossed at the ankle, not the knee. Shoulders back—when they're hunched forward, it indicates a lack of interest or feelings of inferiority.

- **Lean:** Lean forward slightly (without hunching your shoulders, of course) as a sign of interest.

- **Eye contact:** Unless you're working in a culture where eye contact is inappropriate, look your listener in the eye frequently. Avoid staring by looking from one eye to the other, and "smile" with your eyes. If you have a tendency to look off into space or close your eyes while thinking and talking, work with a friend to correct this habit. Relax and smile (with both your mouth and your eyes). If asked a difficult question, keep your eye contact steady. Glancing away or not looking into your manager's eyes as you answer can be interpreted as a sign of untruthfulness.

- **Eyebrows:** Relax your eyebrows—tension in eyebrows indicates confusion, stress, or fear.

- **Mouth:** Mind your mouth! Downward turns or flat lines in the mouth can put people off, while a smile or upward turns in the mouth indicate that you welcome interaction.

- **Head:** Keep head movements to a minimum. Nod occasionally to indicate that you're listening.

- **Arms and hands:** Arms crossed indicates that you are protecting your body. Fidgeting with fingers or a pen indicates that you are agitated or bored, or possibly that you are anxious to say something. Remember to keep your hands below your shoulders—no touching the face, nose, or ears; no rubbing your chin; no scratching your head; and so on.

- **Gestures:** To emphasize your key points, consider small hand gestures. When your manager is speaking, keep your body still as a sign that you are listening intently.

- **Personal distance:** Be attuned to individuals' personal space— the distance is different for everyone. Try this test: Walk toward a business colleague and maintain eye contact as you move closer. The second you cross into the person's boundary of personal space, their eyes will dart away, telling you you've gotten too close.

- **Nervous activity:** Physical tension in the body may present itself in the form of nail-biting, chewing gum, grinding teeth, jiggling a leg or foot, playing with hair, or scratching an ear (always keep your hands away from your face and below your shoulders). One trick for channeling nervous energy that won't be noticed by your manager is to drive the fingernail from your index finger into the flesh of your thumb on the same hand. Press to the point of creating pain. You'll find it difficult to carry on other, more noticeable nervous movements at the same time!

Offer Supporting Documentation

Assemble supporting documentation. Going into your promotion conversation without it is akin to a door-to-door salesman trying to sell a wonder cleaner without showing you that it works. Supporting documentation will help your manager see the return on investment and show her you're serious.

Items in your arsenal of supporting documentation can include the following:

- The "Before-After-and-Beyond" Position Description
- Competency and Contributions Addendum
- Proposal
- Up-to-date Internal Resume or Personal Brand Documents

Before describing some of this documentation, let me insert a caveat. You must use your intuition about how much documentation to prepare for your manager. Some managers will be impressed to see a tome of material. Others will be overwhelmed. Your best bet is to have material ready, recognizing that you may not need (or have the opportunity) to present all of it. See the suggestions later in this section about when to use your documentation.

Before-After-and-Beyond Position Description

One of the best documents you can prepare is a Before-After-and-Beyond Position Description. To do so, create a table with a three-column format. In the first column, list your current job descriptions. In the second column, comment on how you are meeting and exceeding those responsibilities. In the third column, identify the "Above & Beyond" initiative and responsibilities you have taken on. This allows your manager to quickly see that you are already doing some or all of a higher-level role. Table 4.2 illustrates the Before-After-and-Beyond Position Description.

Table 4.2: Before-After-and-Beyond Position Description

Current Responsibilities	Progress on Current Responsibilities	"Above and Beyond" Initiative and Contributions
[Example] Create brochures.	Exceeding expectations— generated 20 percent more than anticipated.	Made brochures interactive and available online for customer access. Doing so has increased add-on sales of product B by 23 percent.
[Example] Interface with outsourced vendors.	Improved communications by making onsite visits to our two key vendors and communicating expectations. Doing so has helped eliminate their past history of missing deadlines.	Created Web-based interface tool that allows for instant communication between team members in multiple locations.

MY BEFORE-AFTER-AND-BEYOND POSITION DESCRIPTION

Use this worksheet to create your own Before-After-and-Beyond Position Description.

Current Responsibilities	Progress on Current Responsibilities	"Above and Beyond" Initiative and Contributions
_____	_____	_____
_____	_____	_____
_____	_____	_____
_____	_____	_____
_____	_____	_____
_____	_____	_____
_____	_____	_____
_____	_____	_____
_____	_____	_____
_____	_____	_____
_____	_____	_____
_____	_____	_____
_____	_____	_____

Make the Before-After-and-Beyond Position Description a part of your Career Coups file (a file that contains letters of appreciation, kudos and attaboys, statistical data substantiating your accomplishments, and more). Update the Before-After-and-Beyond Position Description on a monthly basis or as often as needed to ensure your accomplishments aren't forgotten. Keeping this information at your fingertips will make it a snap to update a resume or online career portfolio, prepare for performance reviews, submit information for a promotion, remind your manager of your recent contributions, or introduce yourself to a new manager.

Competency and Contributions Addendum

As mentioned earlier in this chapter, many larger companies identify specific competencies for every position as a means of measuring skill and progress. Once you're clear on the competencies for your current and target position, create a document that identifies specific accomplishments you've contributed relevant to each competency.

For example, this product design manager for an apparel manufacturer needed to prove her competencies in the areas of fabric design, wash development, sell-through, and technology (among others). Her Competency Addenda looked, in part, like figure 4.1.

Competencies & Contributions

Fabric Design

- Worked with mills to create new patterns and qualities on a seasonal basis.
- Identified new mills in Pacific Rim.
- Earned company's "Excellence Awards" twice for fabric design initiatives.

Wash Development

- Continuously created new wash techniques and formulas.
- Formulas were adopted by other departments, including Tops and Activewear.

Sell-Through

- Developed lines that exceeded objective with sell-throughs of 90% to over 100% at wholesale.

Technology

- Represented department on global Web technology project and contributed to program development and testing.
- Served as department's technical resource during implementation.

Figure 4.1: A sample Competency Addendum.

This next example in figure 4.2 shows competencies and contributions in the areas of strategy, finance, operations, and product development for an investment management executive.

To help identify accomplishments for your Competency & Contributions document, use the SMART Story™ worksheet earlier in this chapter. You can create a Competencies & Contributions document similar to the samples in figures 4.1 and 4.2 by transferring the "Results" section from your various SMART Stories™.

Competencies & Contributions Summary

Strategy

- Identified opportunities in strong, weak, or uncertain market conditions and leveraged firm resources to gain differentiation and immediate traction, doubling sales in the past 12 months.

- Collaborated with executive teams to craft and execute three core initiatives involving differentiation, product-line evolution, product positioning, acquisition integration, and internal restructuring.

- Led startup strategy that delivered 91% growth in AUM within 9 months.

Finance

- Managed 8-figure operating budgets at or under budget.

- Partnered with CFO to enhance management planning, budgeting/tracking, and profitability analysis.

- Established line-item budgeting and held regional managers accountable for expense budget planning and control.

Operations

- Managed staff of 65. Set higher expectations across-the-board for rep/customer service, technology capabilities, processing, and reporting standards. Improved our record of regulatory compliance.

- Reconfigured client statements and designed sales reporting system, accommodating data from 2 distinct collection systems. Improved processing from 89% to 99%+ error-free processing.

- Merged 3 sales teams and product lines with recent acquisition. Led seamless relocation from Southern California to Pacific Northwest (still maintaining award-winning customer and financial advisor service levels).

- Coordinated with Chief Counsel on prospectus changes/filings, stickers, and proxy votes. Gained NASD concessions on sales materials and performance disclosure issues. Prepared and presented materials to Board.

- Researched and addressed regulatory issues affecting distribution of mutual funds in Canada and the EU.

Product Development

- Worked with Product Development Team on pricing and integration of 20 additions into existing product line.

- Teamed with internal staff on development and introduction of new multi-manager asset allocation funds, raising more than $800 M in first year of operation.

Figure 4.2: A sample Competency Addendum for an investment management executive.

Proposal Letter

In some cases, your best strategy may be a proposal letter. This letter, based on a strategy developed by career coach Barb Poole, CCMC, CPRW, CERW, BS of www.HireImaging.com, shows how you might lay out a promotion proposal to your manager.

Samples of other position proposals and internal resumes can be found in appendix D.

GETTING YOUR DOCUMENTS TOGETHER

Identify which personal marketing documents will best support your candidacy.

- Before-After-and-Beyond Position Description

- Competency and Contributions Addendum

- Proposal

- Up-to-date Internal Resume, Accomplishments Summary, or Personal Brand Documents

When will you prepare these and/or what support will you need to create dynamite documents? _____

_____

For a complete resource on preparing resumes, see the third edition of *Résumé Magic* (JIST Publishing). For a list of cream-of-the-crop career/resume specialists who hold the designation of Master Resume Writer, go to the Career Masters Institute site at www.cminstitute. com/cgi-bin/mrw-list.cgi.

When to Use Your Documentation

When should you share your supporting documentation? As mentioned earlier, use good judgment. Do not bombard your manager straight out of the chute with all your material. Instead, have it ready in a folder (or in an online portfolio) and pull out appropriate items as the discussion moves along.

Tip: *Ready to create an online portfolio for your career? Check out the resources at www.Brandego.com and www. BlueSkyPortfolios.com.*

Sheila Smart

123 East Street
Sunnyvale, FL 34567
ssmart@americalcorp.com

[date]

Dear Ms. Manager:

Thanks for accompanying me on the Johnson & Johnson onsite visit last week. Your presence allowed the purchasing team to truly see the commitment our company is putting behind its products.

Likewise, I appreciate the commitment you've shown toward my professional development over the years with Americal Corporation. It's been a pleasure to work and grow under your leadership. On the return flight, I mentioned briefly some of the ideas I had for growing the business. You sounded very receptive to those ideas and confirmed that they align with the organization's strategic direction.

I'd like to keep the momentum going and discuss this in more detail, as well as briefly review my performance and role at our follow-up meeting next Monday. To help you prepare for that discussion, I've included some highlights below.

Recent Contributions

- **Revenue Increase:** Top-producing market manager (President's Club), nearly doubling sales over prior year.
- **Fastest Growing Account:** Managed rapid-growth account increases, selling $3.2M into 26 new warehouses (up from 14 to 40) with exclusive distribution. Analyzed untapped market opportunities to develop business for new warehouses.
- **Financial:** Together with CFO and Director of Finance, crafted a discount package in response to account request. Win-Win: Aided account with a 1% discount and improved company cash flow from 45 to 10 days.
- **Profit:** Delivered margins 2 full percentage points above company average through cost-plus pricing, effective product assortments, and negotiations on delivery requirements, discounts, and support.
- **Sales Forecasting:** Excellent record for forecast accuracy of 95-100% (30 days) and 90-110% (90 days).
- **Visionary Team Builder:** Assembled first Customer Council formed with cooperation of the account's top managers and sales reps. Team shares best practices companywide. Initiative yielded a $1.1 million sales increase.

As market/sales manager, I bring a breadth and depth of expertise to the table in multiple areas:

New Business Development, Sales Management,
Relationship Selling, Consultative Selling, Fact-Based Selling (IRI, AC Nielsen, Polk)
Business Analysis (Retail Link), Forecasting, Category Management
Mass Merchandiser Relationship Management (Wal-Mart, Target, Kmart)
Supply-Chain Model Innovation, Customer Scorecards

In addition, my roles on cross-functional teams have provided exposure to marketing, IT management, quality assurance, new model introductions, and new product initiatives.

I believe that much of the value I bring to Americal Corp is in my ability to strategize and innovate, such as the highly successful Customer Council program; as well as my passion for creating trust-based connections with internal and external customers—relationships that get things done and make things happen.

You know I'm an advocate of action plans! My career plan has always mapped a performance-based path to being in a director role. If there has been one piece not feeling like a good fit for me at Americal Corp, it has been that, while I have been performing many of the responsibilities of a director, I have not formally held the title with its various benefits nor been part of the Executive Team.

Figure 4.3: A sample proposal letter.

Ms. Manager
[date]
Page Two

I have done extensive research on manager-level and director-level positions, assessing my responsibilities, overall accountability, and accomplishments with comparable positions in multiple companies throughout the United States, as well as in comparable geographic areas. It is very important to me to achieve my goal of being part of the Executive Team, and I believe I have earned it. I also respect that you may have questions about this type of change. ***Therefore, after careful thought, I am prepared to make a proposal:***

- I have created an online portfolio of my work, which includes my internal résumé, a "Competencies & Contributions" addenda conveying leadership and successful business strategies used to achieve lucrative results for Americal Corp, my mission and branding statement, endorsements and testimonials from customers at every level from buyers to C-level executives … and more. I know (and appreciate) that you like to see a strong paper-trail on initiatives, so I've taken the time to document my performance to substantiate any rewards I might receive for that performance. Please view the portfolio at www.sheilasmart.com/value.html. I think you'll see that it conveys my unique brand and functional value to Americal Corp and its mission.

- For three months, beginning Monday, I ask that you consider this a trial period. I'm the product—try before you buy. During this period, I would interact with you on a more regular basis. We could meet for 30 minutes each week—you choose the day / time; it can, of course, be more often than that if you prefer.

- I would attend Executive Team meetings—not as a member—but, instead, to demonstrate the value I can bring to the brainstorming and decision-making process.

- At the end of this period, if you feel that I would be an asset to the Executive Team, we would meet to review the results and, being the optimist I am, I believe the next step would be a discussion regarding my transition to Director with appropriate compensation. I want to make it clear that I do not expect any salary increase or additional perks during this trial period.

That's it! There are no catches. I believe this is a win/win scenario, and hope you will agree. You've given me the reins on other ideas in the past that have turned out to be winners, and I appreciate you giving this consideration as well. Thanks again for the opportunity to be part of Americal Corp. I look forward to continued contributions—and great things for Americal!

Respectfully,

Sheila Smart

One coaching client of mine prepared a stunning resume loaded with numbers-driven accomplishments and asked for his director's input on it prior to submitting it for a director-level opening. The director, who had been subtly downplaying my client's skill level to her fellow directors and vice president, was notably impressed. The resume served to help rebrand my client's image from underling to leader and proactive change agent.

Optional: Briefly Touch on Salary

If you want more compensation as part of your promotion plan, you'll need to bring up the subject **sooner rather than later.** This will help your manager recognize that you're not intending to take on a bigger role without some additional compensation.

In larger companies, pay scale will be tied directly to the position title or grade. If you're shooting for a new title with your promotion, an increase in compensation will automatically accompany that, so you may not have to bring up this subject. For companies that don't have a defined pay structure in place, you will need to bring up the topic of compensation during your initial conversation. If you wait until later, it will appear as though you've not been honest from the outset. (Read more about salary negotiations in chapter 6.)

Identify Potential Next Steps

Wrap up your meeting with a clear understanding of what the next steps will be. For example:

> So, to summarize our conversation, Mr. Manager, you'll start the paperwork with HR for the Account Manager title and salary grade, and announce this at the Town Hall meeting. I'll hit the ground running and will give you those status reports each Friday afternoon. My commitment is to support your success in this as well. This is going to be a win-win for both the company and our customers!

Or this example:

> So, to summarize our conversation, Mr. Manager, you'd like me to continue to hone my people management skills, as well as take ownership of the outsourcing project. I understand that we'll revisit this in eight weeks and if I have delivered a 15 percent increase in productivity that you'll formalize my title to Account Manager at a grade 22 salary level.

Language: Carefully Word Your Request

Choose your words wisely! Promotable people use language that is

- Positive, not plaintive
- Respectful, not rude
- Clear, not obscure
- Astute, not obtuse
- Winsome, not whining

These seven tips will help you get off to the right start:

- **Check your emotions:** Be absolutely certain you're approaching from a position of enthusiasm and goodwill (offering a value proposition) and not jealousy, anger, or frustration over not having gotten your fair share.

- **Tone of voice:** Your voice should convey warmth and confidence. One of the best ways to warm up your voice is by caring about the person you are speaking to. If you have a boss who is difficult, think about the positive things that will come from your proposal, such as improved efficiency on the job, more money in the bank, customers who are being serviced better, and so on. Confidence will come from knowing you bring value and a strong ROI to the equation.

- **Pitch:** Your voice has a range of pitch. A high pitch can sound childish, whiny, or nervous. Consciously lower your voice to a comfortable low within your range. To warm up your voice, sing (privately) your favorite song, then take it down a key or two.

- **Contrast:** Vary the pitch and volume of your voice. Just as a musical piece varies in its intensity and frequency to be interesting, so must you.

- **Speed:** Slow down your presentation (but not to a crawl), especially if you have a tendency to talk fast when you're nervous or excited. Pause occasionally, and during those times remind yourself to check your tone of voice.

- **Ar-ti-cu-late:** Be conscious of your tongue working inside your mouth. If people ask you to repeat yourself, you're likely mumbling.

- **Assertive style:** Say it assertively. Communication styles can range from passive and passive-aggressive to aggressive or arrogant. Somewhere in the middle is the perfect balance of assertiveness, with the hallmarks of respect, honesty, confidence, open-mindedness, and direct, straightforward communication.

> **Tip:** *Self-assess your communication style with this quick quiz from Joni Rose (better yet, ask someone else to rate you!): http://trainingpd.suite101.com/article.cfm/communication_styles.*

A Two-Way, Win-Win Dialogue, Not a Monologue

Approach the conversation as a two-way discussion, not a one-way demand. Emphasize your track record and value, as well as your understanding of global organizational goals. Figure 4.4 illustrates how a strategy that combines results with a global perspective will position you as a "Star Contributor."

Clearly, those who focus on their results, including both technical skills and social competency, in combination with the global needs of the organization, are best positioned for promotion.

Without some practice, it's highly unlikely that you will magically find persuasive words that convey the bottom-line company-wide benefit of moving you into an enlarged role. Even Robin Williams, king of improvisation, rehearses! Some people find it helpful to write out what you want to say so that each of the words is well-chosen. Then, rehearse in front of a mirror, paying attention to your facial expressions and body language.

You don't need to memorize a lengthy script, but do have your opening and closing down cold. Imagine you have just 60 seconds to make your case for promotion. To do so, you'll need to have honed your message succinctly—to the point that it would fit on a bumper sticker!

Run your ideas past your coach or mentor to get feedback on how others respond to your phrasing. All of this prep work will add to your comfort level and confidence. One director of an international apparel company said, "If you're stumbling over your words as you're asking for a promotion, it's not going to make a very good impression!"

Potential Contributor	Star Contributor
Description: You understand the big picture and how your performance impacts teams, department, organization, and customers (a component of "Critical Thinking" in the "Top 10 Characteristics of Promotable People" (see chapter 1); however, you may need your skill-set further developed (Competency) and/or confidence boosted (Confidence). **Action Steps:** Fine-tune developmental needs (technical skills and/or social skills); identify your contributions and accumulate small-step victories to increase confidence.	**Description:** You are both productive and have a global perspective. You are strategic about delivering results that align with the organization's key priorities. Star Contributors demonstrate all of the "Top 10 Characteristics of Promotable People": Character, Confidence, Communication, Competency, Connection, Critical Thinking, Contributions, Commitment, Control, and Coach-like.
Uninitiated Apprentice	**Uninformed Producer**
Description: You approach your career from a self-focused perspective (for instance, "What can this company do for me?" instead of "What can I do for the company?"). **Action Steps:** Be open to directive supervision; ensure there's a good job-fit for your strengths/interests; inquire about how your individual work impacts global organizational goals; with respect to the "Top 10 Characteristics of Promotable People," focus on Character, Competency, and Critical Thinking.	**Description:** You are productive, but uninformed about how your results impact the organization. Regarding the "Top 10 Characteristics of Promotable People," you may be strong in Contribution and Character but lack in the Critical Thinking category or Connection category. **Action Steps:** Gain exposure to and an understanding of the organization's global goals; pair up with internal organizational mentors; take advantage of opportunities to work with cross-functional and interdepartmental teams; volunteer for projects outside of your normal sphere.

FOCUS + (global perspective) / − (self-focused orientation)

− (unproductive)   RESULTS   + (high technical/social competency)

Figure 4.4: Star Contributor strategy.

L.I.S.T.E.N. Like a Laser

Something magical happens to a relationship when you listen fully—speakers sense that they are important to you, interesting, valued, and respected. They'll then want to extend to you the same respect. This process is foundational to connecting in conversations with your manager (and peers).

To connect with your manager as you listen, remember these LISTENing tips:

- **L = Laser your focus.** Be fully present: Lock out distractions, look into your manager's eyes, and lean forward slightly to show interest. Concentrate on your manager's comments, not just your piece of the conversation.

- **I = Investigate.** Be curious. Probe beyond the surface…move beyond listening "to" your manager to listening "for" (empathetically) your manager's meaning, motives, feelings, priorities, values, perspective, and needs.

- **S = Silence your tongue!** Hold judgment and listen with an open mind. Don't take things personally. If what your manager is saying makes you defensive, irritated, or nervous, there's a greater chance you'll miss the main point. Let him finish his sentences. Be comfortable with a little silence in the conversation.

- **T = Take brief notes.** If clarification is needed, repeat your manager's question or statement. Take time to formulate your response.

- **E = Elevate the other person.** Good listeners make the other person feel significant, valued, and respected. Act professionally, but resist the urge to be right, show off, or act brilliant with all the right answers. As a candidate for promotion, you're there to contribute to the company's bottom line. Remember the mantra, "It's about them, not me."

- **N = Note the nonverbal.** Mirror the positive body language of your manager. If you perceive body language that indicates stress, confusion, frustration, or boredom, think about how you can respond to improve the situation.

For an informal check on your communication skills, take the 25-Point Communication Check in appendix E.

Emphasize "Progress" More Than "Promotion"

Although the term *promotion* may seem like straightforward language to use when talking to your boss, use the term sparingly! Many a manager interviewed for this book cautioned against using the phrase, "I'd like a promotion" or "I want to get promoted." Why?

1. First, it can put your manager on the defensive, leading him to think, "I don't have it in the budget right now, so I'm just going to say no."

2. Second, if you mention a promotion before the manager sees the corresponding benefit to the company, he may have little motivation to hear you out. There's wisdom in leading with benefits.

3. Finally, promotion means different things to different people, as you saw in chapter 1. It's better to be specific about the progress you want (more responsibility, more money, different title) than to simply ask for a promotion.

> **Tip:** *If you leave the compensation piece out of the initial conversation but revisit it later, it might be misinterpreted as whining. Set expectations for salary in the initial conversation.*

Borrow Language from Sample Conversations

Sometimes it's helpful to hear how others have languaged the promotion conversation. When reading through these samples, underline or highlight phrasing that might be appropriate to your situation.

In the following scenario, the individual anchors her promotion plan around a critical project within the company.

> Thanks for your time. Before I jump in with my ideas, I'd like to make sure I'm on the same page with your vision for the Walker project. Could you say a little bit about how you'd define "extreme success" on that project?

[The manager defines success.]

> And where do you see the greatest need?

[The manager describes the needs, which the employee is already aware of based on research and strategy sessions with her coach/mentor. She responds…]

> I hear you. And I also had some thoughts about how we could make sure that happens. I've been looking at the numbers, and it appears we can boost our returns by 6 to 8 percent if we…

[The employee describes a couple of bullet points and then waits for feedback from the manager. She then continues…]

> I'd like to be the one to take the ball and run with this, because it also fits nicely with some of my personal career goals, one of which includes moving up to a position where I can have a greater impact on strategy and the bottom line, as well as take my compensation to the next level…

[This makes it clear that the employee is not simply raising her hand to take on more responsibilities without some form of compensation.]

[The manager then gives the nod to go ahead, at which time role and salary are discussed. If the manager turns down the salary increase, consider something like this…]

I respect your position on that. I'd like an opportunity to prove myself. Give me 90 days to show you what I can do. If at the end of 90 days I'm successful, compensate me the difference back to our start date. This way, there's no risk for the company. Our client wins, the company wins, and my goals are met as well.

Here is more language that can be helpful in your discussions.

When the company is growing:

It's exciting to see all the plans on the table for continued growth. I've been thinking about how I could contribute and also grow my career with the company.

When the company is contracting:

At this juncture in the company's history, it's critical that we jump-start our sales. Your strategy to market to the vendor community is right on the mark. As an add-on to that, I thought we could also... [explain the strategies] and here is the return on investment we can anticipate. You'll need someone you trust who can take the reins on this. My performance on the recent Search Initiative really honed my skills in this area. I could...

If there is resistance to your proposal:

What do you need to support the fact that this is the right business decision?

Then go about delivering it!

Remember Your Manager's Managers

Depending on the number of management levels within your organization, your manager may need to get input or approval from her counterparts or superiors. Consider this factor in your proposal, and include comments such as this:

I understand that the Customer Service and Order Fulfillment managers will need to be on board with this proposal. I drafted a few talking points on how we can approach them and show the ROI to their departments.

or

Ms. Manager, what do you need to be able to confidently present this to your vice president? I'd like to be in that meeting to support you and offer details on any specific questions that might come up.

or

When could we get the three of us together to talk about this?

If you're presenting a proposal to a group of individuals with more seniority than you and your immediate manager is among that group, make sure you meet with your manager prior to the big meeting and get approval on what you intend to say about her role, if any. You don't want to say something about her in front of the group that will embarrass her or cause her to correct you. Go into the meeting with your manager as an ally.

> **Tip:** *In his classic pocket guide* How to Get Your Point Across in 30 Seconds or Less *(Pocket, 1990) Milo O. Frank suggests that going to the* right *person is important. True, you must start with your manager (never leapfrog over your manager). However, if your manager's boss is the one who really holds the power to promote you, you have to get him involved in the conversation.*

Say It in Person

According to a 2006 study published in the Journal of Personality and Social Psychology, there's only a 50-50 chance of ascertaining the intended tone of any e-mail message. In the study, 30 pairs of undergraduate students e-mailed each other about mundane topics, such as campus food or the weather. Assuming either a serious or sarcastic tone, one member of each pair e-mailed the statement to his or her partner. The partners then guessed the intended tone. The senders predicted that 80 percent of the time their recipients would correctly interpret the tone. In fact, the recipients got it right only a little over 50 percent of the time. Further, the recipients thought they accurately interpreted the messages 90 percent of the time.

The lesson to be learned? E-mail can be easily misinterpreted. It is meant for quick, simple communication. Save any important conversation for face-to-face meetings.

Keep It Going!

Rarely will you march into your manager's office, communicate your desire for advancement, and be knighted there on the spot. It will take perseverance. To keep the doors open for continued conversation, get permission to revisit the subject at a future date. At the conclusion of the conversation or immediately after, mark your calendar to remind you about following up with your manager. Update the action plan you started in chapter 2 with your intentions and commitments.

Creating momentum is critical. Your ability to persevere will be a sign to your manager that you are, indeed, ready for more responsibility.

Key Points: Chapter 4

- There is a time for every season. You can't expect to reap your harvest before you've planted and watered the seeds.

- Promotions don't happen with communication. Remember to T.A.L.K. it out:

    - **T = Timing:** There will be two steps to the conversation: The first is to request a meeting— ask for one-on-one face-time with your manager; the second is to actually have the "career conversation" to discuss how your career progression will align with the company's goals.

    - **A = Agenda:** Determine the most important items to discuss. Know what you want, as well as what your employer and manager want. Know your value to the organization. Decide on the best strategy to present your proposal to your manager and adapt your presentation to your listener. Offer supporting documentation. Briefly touch on salary. And, finally, identify the potential next steps to keep momentum going.

    - **L = Language:** Carefully word your request. Emphasize words like "career progress" and not "promotion." Check your emotions to be certain you're approaching from a position of value and not desperation. Make sure your tone of voice conveys warmth and confidence. Articulate and speak assertively. Make sure the conversation is a two-way, win-win dialogue and not a monologue.

Tip: *In the book* Crisp: Writing Effective E-Mail, *Revised Edition (Crisp Learning, 2003), author and e-communications expert Nancy Flynn cautions, "Many people treat e-mail too casually, writing comments they would never utter aloud. Play it safe. Do not write anything to or about another that you would not feel comfortable saying face-to-face."*

Flynn adds that 28 percent of employers have disciplined or terminated employees for sending e-mail characterized as menacing, harassing, or discriminatory.

- **K = Keep it Going!:** Before you start the conversation with your manager, think through how you will keep the door open to return to this discussion in the weeks to come. Get agreement from your manager on when you can revisit the subject. Mark your calendar and don't let that date slip by unnoticed. Work out an action plan between now and then so that you have some measurable progress to show your manager.

Chapter 5

Strategies for Promotion Roadblocks: I. C.A.N.

I n the process of executing your promotion plan, you're bound to encounter some roadblocks and detours. Count on them. They are life's way of sending you to the gym to exercise your resiliency muscles. Without roadblocks and challenges, we'd all be soft and flabby. When we meet them head-on, we become stronger and healthier. This chapter is devoted to giving you some muscle to manage any challenge that might present itself.

Before getting into the strategies, I'll introduce the resiliency factor and a concept called the "I. C.A.N." mindset. People with a high degree of resiliency display several common characteristics: They are

- Purposeful
- Confident of their value
- Persevering
- Proactive
- Optimistic
- Empowered, with inner strength
- Anxiety-free
- Balanced
- Diligent about self-care
- An inspiration to others

You can be sure that managers clamor to promote people with these characteristics.

Being resilient doesn't require perfect and unwavering self-confidence, just the skills to regain it in the least amount of time possible. Henry Ford said, "Whether you believe you can do a thing or not, you're right." If you believe you can be resilient, you will be.

The "I. C.A.N." Mindset

When operating in full force, your resiliency factor will enable you to say, "I *CAN* do this." And, indeed, you *can* do it when you apply this meaning to the I. C.A.N. acronym:

- **I = Inspire Daily:** Recall a time when you felt utterly inspired, ready to take on the world, confident that everything would work out for the best. What would your career be like if you could have that feeling on a daily basis? Tasks would get tackled immediately, people would want to have you on their team, ideas would flow, and energy would be focused on what really matters. Successful people master the art of recharging themselves with daily inspiration.

- **C = Control the Controllables:** One of the secrets of resilient people is that they concentrate on what they can control. You *can't* control how your manager will respond to your promotion plan. You *can* control how you respond to your manager, and the manner in which you convey your return on investment. You *can't* control whether your manager will go to bat for you in endorsing you to his boss. You *can* control getting on the radar screen of his boss by volunteering for projects that will give you more visibility, weaving your personal stamp into materials that will be seen by the manager's boss, asking to attend meetings where the boss will be present, and so on. People who have a sense of control in their day-to-day lives experience less stress.

- **A = Act Now:** Do not wait to do something that could be done now. This is especially true for actions that put us out of our comfort zone. What do you have a tendency to procrastinate on? Those are the very items that need to be acted on immediately. Why? Because doing so builds self-discipline. Self-discipline brings more self-control. Self-control allows you to act from a position of power and make wise choices that will move you forward. Forward movement builds

> **Tip:** *Who's in charge of your success? Psychologists use the term "locus of control" to describe a person's beliefs about whether internal or external forces are responsible for his success or failure. People with an internal locus of control believe that success is contingent on what they do; those with an external locus of control believe that events outside their personal control determine success. To assess your beliefs, take the free assessment online at www.dushkin.com/ connectext/psy/ch11/ survey11.mhtml.*

momentum, which makes it easier to act. Now the cycle is complete, and you're on a roll!

- **N = Never Give Up!:** Motivational speaker and sales coach Joe Girard aptly stated: "The elevator to success is out of order. You'll have to use the stairs…one step at a time." Perseverance is a key characteristic of someone with resiliency. When your manager gives you a "no," ask, "What would it take to make it yes?" Then go do it. When you hit a roadblock, ask yourself, "What new behavior or way of thinking can I learn from this?" Then go practice it. No's and roadblocks are "double-dip" opportunities—you not only master some new skill in the process, but you deepen your ability to persevere.

Victim or Victor: Turning Adversity into an Advantage

When faced with significant stress, what causes some people to shrivel in defeat while others thrive and find victory? A 12-year study conducted by psychologist Salvatore R. Maddi, Ph.D., followed 400 executives, managers, and supervisors who were downsized by Illinois Bell Telephone as part of one of the biggest deregulation and divestiture cases in American history.

Maddi's results showed that approximately two-thirds suffered significant performance, leadership, and health declines as a result of the extreme stress from the deregulation and divestiture, including heart attacks, strokes, obesity, depression, substance abuse, and poor performance reviews.

However, the other one-third actually thrived during the cataclysmic change. These employees maintained their health, happiness, and performance and felt renewed enthusiasm, despite experiencing the same circumstances as their coworkers.

What gave the thriving group such resilience? Three key attitudes:

- **Commitment:** A sort of "personal pledge" to stay involved in ongoing events, instead of becoming isolated.

- **Control:** The initiative to influence outcomes and not lapse into passivity and powerlessness.

- **Challenge:** A perspective that viewed changes, whether positive or negative, as opportunities for new learning.

Which of the preceding three areas are you strongest in? Which area would you like to focus on improving?

Read more about the study at www.psychologymatters.org/hardiness.html.

15 Common Roadblocks

In the pages that follow, I've catalogued some common roadblocks found on the path to promotion. You'll see commonalities in some of the underlying concerns, which typically point to problems with the boss's behavior or in some cases budget limitations. As you read through, highlight or checkmark those items that might apply to you, as well as tips you'll act on to improve your situation.

#1: You Are Too Valuable in Your Current Role

Potential Issues or Underlying Concerns

❏ Manager seems to be stalling.

❏ Manager doesn't want to lose you as a producer.

Help-in-a-Hurry Tips

- Create your own succession plan if one doesn't already exist. If you haven't been training one or more people to step into your role, get busy. Who are the best candidates to fill your shoes so that you can move up?

> **Tip:** *Recognize your contribution to the problem. In* Managing Up: 59 Ways to Build a Career-Advancing Relationship with Your Boss *(AMACOM/ American Management Association, 1999), Michael and Deborah Singer Dobson offer suggestions for dealing with problem bosses. Consistent with the Control the Controllables concept, they advise looking at yourself and the potential impact your actions may be having on the problem. That doesn't mean you are causing the problems. Instead, the Dobsons point out that you have more power to change yourself than you do your manager. Therefore, responding more effectively is often your most powerful tool.*

- Propose a mentoring plan where you'll get your promotion but also be available to your successor for a set period of time.

- If you sense your manager doesn't want to lose you and you would still report to him in a new promoted role, emphasize your continued support of him. For instance, "I am committed to supporting you as we move this project forward and will continue to give you 100 percent effort so that you also meet your production goals." Or, "I can assure you that a key priority for me is to make sure you look good when it comes to turning in numbers for our district." Continue to act supportive and produce results.

#2: Your Manager Won't Endorse You for Promotion

Potential Issues or Underlying Concerns

❏ Manager won't endorse you to other executives involved in the hiring decision.

❏ Manager doesn't want to lose control, influence, or power over you.

❏ Manager is not completely convinced that you will perform well in the new position, which could reflect on her performance record.

❏ Manager is concerned that you will outshine her if promoted.

❏ Manager either states directly that you're not ready or avoids telling you you're not ready for promotion. (This may or may not be true.)

Help-in-a-Hurry Tips

• Ask specifically about the timeline: "You mentioned that increasing my management skills is a prerequisite to promotion. I'd like to be clear on what you anticipate and how we'll measure success so that I have clear goals."

• If you sense your manager isn't sold on endorsing you in the new position, ask, "What would you need to see in my performance to assure you that this move would benefit the company?"

• If your manager continues to seem evasive about career conversations, watch for an opportune moment to explore this further. Do so in a curious, nonjudgmental tone so that the manager doesn't get defensive or feel backed into a corner. For example, "You know, Mr. Manager, I hear you saying you support me in developing my career, and yet it doesn't seem that much is happening despite my meeting every goal you've set. Help me understand what the benefits are to tapping on the brakes like this."

#3: There Are Limited Opportunities for Promotion

Potential Issues or Underlying Concerns

❏ Your career and the position you're currently in will only be what you make it. Take ownership of your initiative.

Help-in-a-Hurry Tips

- Ask your manager about plans for growth and how you can contribute to that growth.

- Create your own opportunities. Start by looking for problems that need to be fixed and issues that need to be solved. Once you do, find a solution that you can be involved in and identify the return on investment associated with that solution. Voilà, you have a proposal that could lead to promotion.

- Look for projects that interest you and will expand your skill set. There is no shortage of opportunity in the world.

#4: Another Employee More Senior Than You "Needs" to Be Promoted Before You

Potential Issues or Underlying Concerns

- ❏ Politics are at play.

- ❏ There may be a more senior employee who is not as capable as you who your manager owes a favor or who may respond negatively if she isn't promoted first.

Help-in-a-Hurry Tips

- Enlist the support of an advocate who can endorse you to the powers that be and ask, "Who made up the rule that we have to promote a more senior employee first? John is a better producer and a better leader. We don't want to risk losing him because of rules that aren't serving us well."

- Within your promotion proposal, suggest a solution that allows the person with more seniority to also "win" with, for instance, a new title that gives the person some perk or special task.

- If you are truly the best person for the job, have a courageous conversation with your manager and ask in a curious, nonjudgmental tone of voice, "Help me understand how that policy best serves the company in this situation."

#5: Your Manager Doesn't Perceive You as a Logical Choice for Promotion

Potential Issues or Underlying Concerns

❏ Manager is grooming someone else or has a favorite who is the "heir apparent" for promotion.

❏ Manager seems oblivious that you are interested in promotion.

Help-in-a-Hurry Tips

• Make certain the manager knows your career development goals.

• If necessary, have a courageous conversation with your manager that covers what you've accomplished and where you see yourself in the months or years to come. "Ms. Manager, my intentions for my career involve contributing in the role of Account Supervisor in the next 8 to 12 months, and then Account Manager beyond that. My salary goals are to generate contributions to the company that warrant a salary in the $70,000 to $80,000 range within the next three years. I've mapped out some ideas for how to make that happen, and would welcome your suggestions."

Articulating your goals will create a new reality for your manager. Once those seeds are planted, continue to take action, deliver results that will validate your qualification in your manager's eyes, and follow up at appropriate intervals.

• Request specific assignments and volunteer for projects that will increase the experiences and skill sets needed to be promoted.

#6: You Are Too New to the Company to Be Promoted, or Not Known by the Right People

Potential Issues or Underlying Concerns

❏ You don't have the depth of organizational knowledge needed to excel.

❏ You'll upset the apple cart by being promoted earlier than more senior individuals (also see strategies under "Another Employee More Senior Than You 'Needs' to Be Promoted Before You").

Help-in-a-Hurry Tips

- Meet and greet everyone you can. Find an informal guide within the company who can introduce you to key players.

- Volunteer for projects that would put you on the radar screen of the right folks. (For a great success story, see the sidebar, "Getting on the Radar Screen: Volunteer and Be of Value.")

- If you are in a company with a complex organizational structure, develop relationships with those who have the power to promote by asking for a few minutes of their time. Always be cautious to follow the chain of command to make sure your immediate supervisor is aware of, and okay with, your activity. For instance, you might say to your immediate supervisor, "Betty, I'd like to share with John some of the wins our team has had and wanted to get your input on the appropriate way to approach him." For example, if "John" is someone a level above your manager, you might say, "John, I was speaking with Betty the other day and she suggested you might appreciate seeing some of the wins our project team has had recently. And I'd value your input on some of our other projects as well. I wondered where you might have a few minutes in your schedule in the coming weeks." This makes it clear to John that you have Betty's okay and aren't trying to sidestep protocol.

Getting on the Radar Screen: Volunteer and Be of Value

Ann was hired as a district manager for a pharmaceutical company. She quickly noted a weakness in the company's process for reviewing resumes and gained agreement from the training department that this was an area they could improve on. Ann enlisted the support of a resume expert who created a PowerPoint presentation to teach managers how to analyze resumes for credible contributions and potential liabilities.

This earned the attention of the training department, which needed people to help write training modules for senior district managers. Ann offered, "I'd be happy to help," and in doing so, met Jerry, the person who was the lead on the project.

Soon after that, Jerry mentioned to Ann, "I might be interested in you as a manager-in-residence" (a prize position, normally reserved for district managers with three to four years of seniority with the company). Ann replied, "I'd like that; when would you like me to follow up with you?"

Ann was selected for the coveted manager-in-residence program only six months after being hired—this was unheard of in the company's history.

#7: You Have a Passive or Unskilled Manager Who Takes No Interest in Your Career Development

Potential Issues or Underlying Concerns

❑ You've tried having courageous conversations with your manager about your career development, but to no avail.

❑ In this case, you should have concerns about your manager. (Commit to succeeding in spite of him and, when you're his boss in the years to come, remember to thank him for the extra career coping skills you developed because of him!)

Help-in-a-Hurry Tips

- Look for opportunities to be transferred to another manager.

- Find an internal mentor who will take an interest in your career. Your commitment and enthusiasm will often be a rewarding payback for your mentor's investment of time in you.

- Speak with human resources and ask for their input on the situation.

- Get on the radar screen of executives above your manager (see "You Are Too New to the Company to Be Promoted, or Not Known by the Right People").

- If you think, "I could be doing his job better than he is," it may be true. Keep doing an excellent job (along with the other suggestions related to this roadblock). Time is a great leveler.

#8: You Have a Difficult Relationship with Your Manager

Potential Issues or Underlying Concerns

❑ We all have certain people whom we easily connect with, and a few we don't. There may come a time in your career when you work with a manager who falls into the latter category.

❑ There may be a misunderstanding or situation that needs to be addressed.

❑ There may be concerns by executives above your manager that if you can't get along with this person, who else will you not be able to get along with?

Help-in-a-Hurry Tips

- Take the perspective that this is an opportunity to learn how to work with a challenging individual. Set appropriate boundaries, be professional at all times, and focus on delivering results instead of trying to win over your manager.

- If your manager causes you to get easily frustrated or angry, recognize how the manager may be pushing your buttons. Once you know the triggers, you can teach yourself to be aware of them and respond in a more effective manner.

- Look past the irritation to the need. Allow your manager to be human and fallible, just like all of us. There's power in forgiveness.

- If something happened to cause a previously strong relationship to go south, strategize with your mentor or coach. It may be that an apology is in order. Or it may be that giving up your need to be right (even if you are right) would repair the rift.

- If your manager is discriminating or harassing you, you need to objectively document the situation and report it to human resources.

#9: Your Manager Is Taking Credit for Your Ideas

Potential Issues or Underlying Concerns

❑ Your manager has a big ego and may be thinking, "You're under my supervision, so it's only fair that I get credit for developing you." In some respects, she's right.

❑ Your manager is afraid you will outshine her.

Help-in-a-Hurry Tips

- Let your manager take credit for a few of your accomplishments. You will be less of a threat to her if you do. Choose your battles wisely.

- Offer compliments to feed her ego. Of course, they must be sincere, so watch for activities she does well. For instance, "Jean, I couldn't help but be impressed with the way you handled the vendor negotiations. That was an amazing move at the end where you got them to agree to free shipping. That'll make our budget numbers look great!"

- Watch for opportunities in meetings to say things like, "I am really appreciative that Manager Mike gave me the opportunity on this project to 'take the ball and run with it.' It's been a very rewarding experience to see the results roll in…." This subtly makes it known that you had the lead.

> **Tip:** *In her national bestseller* Nice Girls Don't Get the Corner Office *(Warner Business Books, 2004), Lois P. Frankel, Ph.D., gives insightful wisdom into what meetings are really about. "Most meetings are an incredible waste of time if you think the content is what they're all about. It's not. Meetings are to see and be seen, meet and greet, or play show-and-tell."*

- E-mail your new ideas to your boss but cc other managers who may have some interest in the project. In your e-mail, mention "Mr. Manager, I'm cc'ing Manager Mary because it could also impact her team positively should you decide to implement this."

- Share your new ideas in meetings so that others are aware of where the ideas originally came from. Be cautious that, when sharing, you don't say something that embarrasses or catches your manager off guard; you never want to make him uncomfortable in front of his peers.

- Put your name, as well as your manager's name if appropriate, on reports or other documents that have your thought leadership. For example,

Outsourcing Proposal & Return on Investment Projections

Prepared by John Q. Smith

Jane Doe, Manager, Procurement Department

- If it's not possible to include your name on a report that will be seen by people with the power to promote you, consider mentioning your involvement in e-mails or other correspondence associated with the report. Your goal here is not to grandstand but to casually reference your contributions to the team. Mentioning other people's contributions is a way to share the spotlight and still get your name in the picture.

#10: You Are Attempting Too Big a Move

Potential Issues or Underlying Concerns

❏ Most managers are very cautious about handing over power, and with good reason. If you fail, they look bad.

❏ The manager may think that you aren't savvy enough to see the benefits that come from patient, steady progress.

❏ The manager may think that you haven't yet "paid your dues."

Help-in-a-Hurry Tips

• Think big, but be realistic and strategic. For instance, if you have a big idea that you're convinced would work for the company, share the big idea, but offer a phased process of implementation that would ensure success. No company is going to invest in a big new project without some kind of pilot program.

• Look at the sequence of positions other successful people have taken to get where you want to be. Are you leaving out any steps? If so, what are the drawbacks of missing out on those experiences? What experiences can you substitute to address your manager's potential concerns?

#11: You Have Had Poor Performance Evaluations or Been Turned Down for Promotion

Potential Issues or Underlying Concerns

❏ You were associated with a project that didn't go well.

❏ You said or did something that caused people to question your credibility, motives, or professionalism.

❏ You have not met performance expectations on past evaluations or you had a tough reviewer for your past evaluation.

Help-in-a-Hurry Tips

• If your prior performance evaluation wasn't positive, be extra diligent about documenting your successes. Do this on a weekly basis so that you remember any items that will be in your favor. Send your manager a short e-mail on Friday afternoons recapping the successes for the week. Compile each of these updates into one file on your computer so that you have access to it when it comes time for your next review.

- If you need to do some damage control regarding your reputation, think strategically and bring in help. Talk to your mentor, coach, or manager (if you're on good terms with him) about how to improve your image. Of course, nothing beats producing great results in a humble, team-spirited manner.

- If you were associated with negative circumstances in the past, sometimes the best tactic is to hunker down and not be noticed for anything except exceptional results. The situation may eventually be forgotten as time passes.

#12: There Are Problems with Your Appearance

Potential Issues or Underlying Concerns

❏ In the world of work, few people will be honest with you that you're not getting promoted due to being overweight, having an unkempt appearance, donning an antiquated wardrobe, or even smelling of cigarette smoke (especially noticeable if most of the others in your company don't smoke). Often, the only clue you'll receive is from anonymous feedback on 360° performance evaluations.

❏ Your manager may be concerned that you won't represent the company with the desired image or level of professionalism.

❏ Your manager may be concerned that you're not observant enough to recognize what's expected within your corporate culture or you're not open to change.

❏ If you are a smoker or overweight, there may be concerns that you lack the self-control to quit smoking or lose weight. And if you can't, what other business areas might this lack of self-control spill into? (Note: Although these concerns may be ungrounded, they can still be perceived concerns. Perception is reality!)

Help-in-a-Hurry Tips

- Review any 360°-type assessments for comments that allude to any of the preceding concerns. If your organization hasn't used an internal 360° assessment, ask your manager about conducting your own research on your personal brand.

> **Tip:** *If you're in the market for an image update, enlist the support of an expert. One of my trusted authorities on the subject is Mary Ann Dietschler (www.CoachMaryAnn. com).*

- Ask a mentor or someone you trust (preferably someone successful inside your company) to be honest with you about what might need to change. For instance, "If there were one thing about me personally that might prevent me from getting promoted—even if it were something that people would be hesitant to tell me directly—what would that be?"

- Work with a coach, image consultant, or branding expert to help with a professional makeover.

- Evaluate your wardrobe, hairstyle, glasses, and so on by comparing it to those who are being promoted or are in the position you'd like to hold. Make any necessary adjustments. You don't need to clone yourself to a star performer, but you do need to fit into the corporate culture.

- If wardrobe is the primary concern, shop at a store that specializes in business attire and ask for help. Tell them that you are working on your promotion plan and want to be sure your wardrobe is appropriate for the type of position you're targeting.

- If weight is the primary concern, ensure that your clothing is figure-flattering, of good-quality material, and cut generously (don't try squeezing into a smaller size just to flatter your ego). Again, assistance from someone who knows the ins and outs of fashion will be helpful. You may feel silently judged for being overweight; if so, curb any temptation to retaliate. Instead, focus on your positive personality and ability to produce results.

  Of course, losing weight is always a good idea from a health standpoint, but don't beat yourself up for overeating. That usually just causes you to turn to food again for comfort. If you find yourself eating for any reason other than hunger, ask yourself, "What do I truly need to do to take care of myself right now?" It may be a simple self-care action, such as removing yourself from the stress you're under for 10 minutes, grabbing a quick nap in your car during lunch, or even taking care of some responsibility that's been hanging over you.

- Women, be cautious to not dress suggestively, as this can cause management to question your judgment.

#13: Your Communications/Presentation Style Needs Improvement

Potential Issues or Underlying Concerns

❑ If you can't communicate persuasively, how will you influence direct reports, upper management, customers, clients, or the public?

Help-in-a-Hurry Tips

- Join Toastmasters or work with an individual skilled at delivering polished presentations and persuasive communications.

- Communicating and presenting are physical activities. There is no way to get better without practicing—it won't be accomplished by silently rehearsing in your head. Practicing aloud gets it into your muscle memory.

- When making presentations, pause occasionally to collect your thoughts and remember to breathe. Find a friendly face in the audience (or ask a trusted colleague ahead of time to be your cheerleader who silently nods in agreement and smiles at appropriate times); look to this person frequently to help keep you centered.

- To quell any performance jitters, focus on whether your audience is getting what it needs—you can't think about yourself and the audience at the same time!

- When preparing for informal meetings, review materials to refresh your memory and jot down bulleted talking points to help keep you focused.

#14: You Need to See the Global Perspective of Your Organization

Potential Issues or Underlying Concerns

❑ You don't understand how your position intersects with others or how it contributes to the bottom line.

❑ You have a self-focused agenda.

Help-in-a-Hurry Tips

- Start off each day with a checklist of priorities. At the top of that checklist, write "see the big picture" to remind you to think about the global perspective and how you can contribute to it.

- Volunteer for projects that will give you exposure to more than what you normally see in your day-to-day work.

- Ask for input and feedback from individuals in other departments.

- Network internally and externally— challenge yourself to meet new people who can add to your perspective.

- Ask your manager how your department fits into the bigger picture and how it contributes to the bottom line (but be careful not to ask your manager something you should already know).

> **Tip:** *Don't alienate yourself by missing the global perspective! An executive with a 1,300-employee organization recalled how one manager absolutely hung himself in a meeting when he stood up and spoke of a strategic plan for his IT department. The plan made no connection to the organization's needs or the customer's needs, and there was no reference whatsoever about the resources required for deployment. It was just "cool" technology that the manager was excited about. Everyone in the room was flabbergasted with this individual's self-absorption and lack of a global perspective.*

#15: Your Confidence Needs a Boost

Potential Issues or Underlying Concerns

❑ Managers will not entrust important projects or budgets to someone who is sheepish, shrinking, or overly self-conscious.

❏ You will not be given supervisory responsibilities, as employees don't follow someone who is always uncertain or second-guessing themselves.

Help-in-a-Hurry Tips

- One of the fastest ways to boost your confidence is to experience some sort of a win. To do so you'll need to get moving—wins are virtually impossible without action. Start small and tackle some little task that you've been putting off. Choose something you can do in the next 10 minutes. Do it now.

- Once you have a few warm-up wins under your belt, you'll have the emotional energy to tackle some bigger tasks. Choose something important to your manager's priorities.

- Now up the ante by asking your manager for a challenging assignment. She will sense your newfound confidence and, if she's a good manager, she will want to foster it.

- Remember that the further the task is from your comfort zone, the greater the confidence you'll experience when completing it. You'll begin to sense you can tackle anything once you've faced down a few of your comfort-zone gremlins (a gremlin is that voice you hear in your head that accuses you of not being able to do something).

> **Tip:** If you choose to pursue a position with another company, choose wisely. Who you work for can make or break the situation. Look for a manager who has a track record of developing and promoting employees. Talk to people who have worked for him in the past. Find out the scuttlebutt. Ask questions. Who you work for can be everything!

- Recall times in your life when you've been at your best. What was present that made this so? What can you control that will allow you to be at your best today?

Know When to Walk Away

Remember that this book is about controlling the controllables. If you have done everything in your power to position yourself as promotable and the company won't or can't meet your career needs, be ready with a Plan B, which might involve a move to another company.

If you decide to look for greener pastures after having pulled together your promotion plan, you'll have quite a bit going for you:

- You will be very marketable to other employers because you have clarified your value, brand, and return on investment.

- You already have many of your personal marketing materials ready to go.

- Your confidence is up because you've been taking action.

Then, it's simply a matter of touching base with your network to explore and evaluate opportunities. (For a complete how-to on interviewing and job search, see my prior books, *Interview Magic* and *Job Search Magic*, published by JIST.)

ROADBLOCK BUSTERS

Use this worksheet to identify roadblocks and help-in-a-hurry tips that will work best in your situation.

Roadblock I need to take action on: #_____

Actions I will take: _____

_____

_____

_____

Roadblock I need to take action on: #_____

Actions I will take: _____

_____

_____

_____

Roadblock I need to take action on: #_____

Actions I will take: _____

_____

_____

_____

Roadblock I need to take action on: #_____

Actions I will take: _____

_____

_____

_____

Key Points: Chapter 5

- Use the "I. C.A.N." mindset, remembering to Inspire Daily, Control the Controllables, Act Now, and Never Give Up.

- Create your own succession plan and train others to step into your role.

- Clarify the reason your manager won't endorse your promotion; then ask what he or she would need to be assured that this move would benefit the company.

- Ask about plans for growth and how you can contribute; look for projects that interest you and will expand your skill set.

- If another employee more senior than you "needs" to be promoted before you, find an internal advocate who can endorse you; suggest a solution that allows the other person to also "win"; or ask your manager to help you understand the policy.

- Make certain the manager knows your career-development goals; have a courageous conversation that covers where you see yourself in the future; request specific assignments and volunteer for projects that will increase the experiences and skill sets needed to be promoted.

- Find someone internally who is well-connected who can be a mentor or informal guide; volunteer for projects that will put you on the radar screen of the right folks; develop relationships with those who have the power to promote.

- If you have a passive or unskilled manager who takes no interest in your career development, look for opportunities to be transferred to another manager; find an internal mentor who will take an interest in your career; speak with someone from human resources and ask for their input on the situation; and get on the radar screen of executives above your manager.

- If you have a difficult relationship with your manager, take the perspective that this is an opportunity to learn how to work with a challenging individual.

- Let your manager take credit for a few of your accomplishments; watch for opportunities in meetings to mention how much you've enjoyed having full responsibility for projects; e-mail new ideas to your boss but cc others; or share ideas in meetings where others are aware of where the ideas came from.

- Think big, but be realistic and strategic; share the big idea, but offer a phased process of implementation; look at the positions other people have taken to get where you want to be.

- Be extra diligent about documenting your successes; consider bringing in a coach or mentor if you need to do some damage control.

- Ask a mentor or someone you trust to be brutally honest with you about what about your appearance might need to change for you to be promoted; act on this without being defensive.

- If your communications style needs improvement, practice aloud.

- Train yourself to look for the big picture; volunteer for projects that will give you more exposure; ask for feedback.

- Set up yourself to experience some sort of a win; once you have a few warm-up wins under your belt, you'll have the emotional energy to tackle some bigger tasks. Ask your manager for a challenging assignment.

- If you have done everything in your power to position yourself as promotable and the company won't or can't meet your career needs, be ready with a Plan B, which might involve moving to another company.

Chapter 6

Salary Negotiations: How to Get Paid for the Work You Really Do

In chapter 1, you identified what a promotion means to you. If it includes a desire for additional income with your newfound responsibilities, read on.

When you play your cards right, it won't be difficult to discuss salary. You must get in the game and speak up. An increase in salary will not come by silently wishing for it. You must communicate your expectations.

Of course, in larger companies where salary scales are aligned with specific titles, promotion to a new title will usually bring the associated compensation. However, even in these cases, there can be a range of several thousand dollars, so you'll want to be sure you get the most you deserve.

This 10-step process will guide you through salary discussions:

1. Memorize the mantra—"it's all about value."

2. Know the market.

3. Know what you want.

4. Ask at the right time.

5. Ask the right person.

6. Collaboratively discuss, don't threaten.

7. Find common ground.

8. Ask for what you want.

9. Anticipate objections.

10. Keep the door open.

The following sections take a look at each of the steps in more detail.

Step 1: Memorize the Mantra—"It's All About Value"

It's all about value. To effectively negotiate an increase in salary, you must first understand your value. You've already done this in chapter 4 (under the heading "Know Your Value," see the worksheet "My Return on Investment Solution"). If you haven't had a chance to complete that worksheet, do so now. You'll need the information to create your value statement.

The examples that follow will help you craft language for your value statement. Notice how each one begins with reference to the employer's priorities and goals, as well as weaves in specific, bottom-line figures using percentages and dollar amounts:

> **Tip:** *"The future belongs to the askers,"* says best-selling author Brian Tracy in his book Get Paid More and Promoted Faster: 21 Great Ways to Get Ahead in Your Career *(Berrett-Koehler Publishers, Inc., 2001). He continues, "The future does not belong to those people who sit back, wishing and hoping that things will improve. The future belongs to those people who step up and ask for what they want. And if they don't get it right away, they ask, again and again, until they do get it." (Great quote!)*

- **Customer Service Representative (promoting to Customer Service Trainer):** I understand the company's priority of customer retention, and I've made that my priority as well. My ability to smooth over ruffled feathers and find solutions to problems helped save one of our key accounts last March—that account generates 40 percent of our sales. Moreover, I've helped train other reps to ask questions of customers so they can make product suggestions—those suggestions have helped boost our average sale per call by 12 percent. That translates to more than $7,800 in sales per day!

- **Maintenance Supervisor (promoting to Manager):** Our strategic plan emphasizes on-time delivery to our customers. That cannot happen unless we deliver in the area of productivity. The technical skills I bring to the organization have contributed significantly to overall productivity. Since I've been in the position, we've upped our production 19 percent and reduced assembly-line downtime from 7.0 to 0.5

hours per week. I understand from the sales team that this improvement translates to nearly $130,000 in sales on a monthly basis.

- **Administrative Staffer (promoting to Administrative Leader):** I know that time means money. That's why I take the initiative on admin details for our projects. In doing so, I've freed up Bill (the senior consultant) to add more than 27 percent to his billable client time. That 27 percent brought in an extra $4,700 in billing last month. In my new role as the lead admin staffer, I'll be training the other admin staff to generate similar results, with a target of approximately $28,350 in additional monthly revenue.

- **Program Supervisor (promoting to Program Manager):** One of our strategic priorities is to make our member companies aware of the value of their association with ABC Healthcare. To that end, I've initiated our first Town Hall meeting to solicit feedback on what our members truly want, started our blog that's getting excellent response, and introduced webinars on hot topics that have been widely attended. From that, we've learned that there's opportunity to upsell live training and we have our product development team working on that right now. Our online member satisfaction surveys tell us that 93 percent of members would re-enroll when their contract is up for renewal. This is a 14 percent increase from the survey conducted before I took on this role.

If you are not privy to specific dollar amounts (perhaps your company is tight-fisted with this information), begin accumulating your own baseline data so that you can manage your progress with facts and figures. In the meantime, go back and do your best to recreate numbers based on your best recollection. If necessary, speak in generalities, such as "I'm confident if you check the numbers, you will find that significant progress was achieved."

MY VALUE STATEMENT

Your payoff for creating a value statement will be confidence—knowing what you're worth is a powerful trump card! Using the prior examples as a springboard, write out your value statement here. Remember to lead off with a sentence that underscores your understanding of what's most important to the company.

_____

_____

_____

_____

_____

_____

_____

_____

Step 2: Know the Market

Your salary request must be rooted in facts. If not, you'll lose credibility with your manager. To get at those facts, do your research. Use online sources and talk to people in the industry. Depending on the size of your company and its policies, it may publish a listing of salary ranges. Ask your human resources department, but don't expect them to go to bat for you as an advocate for a raise. They're not in the business of being a union steward whose job is to negotiate on behalf of its members!

Research Comparable Salaries

First you must lay the groundwork by researching comparable salaries. In this step, you'll want to put together some hard numbers about average compensation for someone with your skills, qualifications, years of experience, industry focus, and geographic location. Do this for *both* your current position and for the target promotion position.

With abundant resources available on the Web, in the library, and through your network, there's no need to rely on just one source for comparable salary data. It's unlikely that you will be able to identify a precise salary for the exact promotion you are targeting, but the more information you have, the more confident you'll feel about negotiating your raise based on "fair market value."

Salary Tools and Surveys

The Internet abounds with tools and resources that will give you detailed information about salary ranges for specific professions in specific geographic areas. Additional resources are available in print publications, both books and periodicals, that you can find at your local library. Your reference librarian can help you find the most precise and most comprehensive sources for your particular field and level. Here are a few to get you started:

- **JobStar.org Gateway** (www.jobstar.org): Click on "Salary Info" for a gateway to hundreds of salary surveys available on the Internet.

- **Salary tools:** The following sites are a good place to start; you can easily find many more by entering the word "salary" into your favorite search engine.

  www.payscale.com
  www.careerbuilder.com
  www.monster.com
  www.salary.com
  www.salaryexpert.com
  www.salarysource.com
  www.wageweb.com

- **Professional associations:** If you are a member of one or more professional associations, contact them directly to ask about salary surveys. Or use the *Encyclopedia of Associations* as a reference to find associations relevant to your field, and then call or visit their Web sites for more information.

- **Specialty sites:** Although salary tools are helpful, they may be too generic for your situation. If your professional association doesn't offer salary surveys, look for specialty sites that address the needs of your industry. For example, www.CareerCoachRD.com specializes in helping dietitians negotiate pay raises and compensation.

- **U.S. Department of Labor,** *Occupational Outlook Handbook:* This resource is a treasure-trove of career information including salary ranges. Explore www.bls.gov/oco/ to find data for your profession.

- **The Riley Guide to Employment Opportunities and Job Resources on the Internet:** This exceptional site includes a comprehensive resource list for salary information (www.rileyguide.com/salary.html) and a separate section on executive compensation (www.rileyguide.com/execpay.html). You will find links to dozens of helpful sites; there is also a review of one of the fee-based salary reports you can purchase on the Web.

> **Tip:** *The Hay system is a point-factor method of job evaluation that measures three factors common to all jobs: know-how, problem solving, and accountability. The classification system focuses on internal job relationships and maintaining internal equity. Many large companies use this system for determining salary and make this information available to their employees.*

Internet Postings and Want Ads

The large job boards such as Monster.com and CareerBuilder.com are also a quick source for some hard salary numbers, so don't overlook these resources, even though you're not necessarily planning to change employers.

Network Contacts

Tap your network to gather information on salary. Of course, you would not want to ask your contact how much he or she makes! One or more of these ideas will allow you to ask without stepping into the forbidden territory of someone's personal financial situation:

- "What type of raises have your colleagues in positions similar to mine received over the past three to four years?"

- "What trends are you seeing in terms of compensation for someone who is moving from the position of program manager to program director?"

- "What's the biggest bonus or pay-for-performance increase you've heard of someone receiving?"

- "Here are some highlights of accomplishments in my current position [list them briefly, including the ROI associated with each]. Given the ability to make this sort of contribution, what kind of salary would that translate to at your company?"

- "Tell me, what's the going rate for someone with my experience at your company? What would a top performer earn?"

- "Does your company offer merit raises, pay-for-performance raises, or some other system?"

- "Beyond COLA (cost of living adjustments), what type of raises does your company give?"

- "What does your company pay for Java programmers with five years of experience?"

- "I've been at the same company so long, I'm out of touch with salary ranges. Can you help me with some general information about what other companies are doing?"

Be sure to talk to your friends who work at large companies. Most large organizations have fixed salary ranges based on job grade, and these tables are often published in an employee handbook.

Recruiters

Recruiters are an excellent source of salary information. They are usually looking for "tight-fit" candidates within very specific salary ranges. If you've worked with a recruiter in the past, touch base and ask for a "market check" on your salary expectations. You might also ask whether the recruiting firm has conducted any salary surveys for your profession. And, be ready! Your recruiter contacts may just have open positions they're trying to fill. If you're not interested in them, you'll score points by offering the recruiters some names of people who would potentially be a good fit.

Put It All Together

Relying on multiple sources means that you will have a wide range of data that, together, should give you a fairly accurate picture of the "going rate" for your profession. Table 6.1 shows a sample of comparative salary data developed by a Web designer.

Table 6.1: Research on Comparative Salary Data			
Source	Low Range	Mid Range	Upper Range
Salary tool: workindex.com/salary/ (national averages)	$46,027	$54,704	$58,315
Salary tool: www.salary.com (national averages)	$45,662	$54,269	$57,853
Salary tool: www.salaryexpert.com (New York/statewide average)	$37,383	$47,798	$56,517
Salary survey: American Institute of Graphic Artists	$40,000	$48,000	$56,700
Print ad: Flash Designer/Graphic Artist (Kansas City Star)	$32,000		$40,000
Online ad: Production Artist (New York)	$57,000		$66,000
Network contact: president, Kansas City Ad Club	$40,000	$45,000	$50,000
Network contact: Acme Corporation, job grade 8	$45,000	$47,500	$50,000
Average	$42,965	$49,544	$54,423

Step 3: Know What You Want

Now that you know the "going rate" for people doing the work you want to do, you can begin to clarify what you want in compensation. Increases may come in one or more of these forms:

- **Merit increase:** A merit raise is based on criteria such as job perform-ance, initiative, and attendance. It looks back at past performance.

- **Pay-for-performance increase:** A pay-for-performance increase is set at the beginning of the year (or other review period) and is paid based on attaining specific performance milestones.

- **Competitive pay increase:** This increase is based on a market approach, with an increase equivalent or similar to what other companies are paying.

- **Bonus:** Although some companies give arbitrary year-end bonuses, a formal bonus system is typically tied to either individual performance or group performance.

- **COLA:** A COLA increase, which stands for Cost Of Living Adjustment, is not a raise but an escalation simply to keep in step with the cost of living.

COMPARE YOUR SALARY

Compare your current salary to your research. Place a checkmark next to the statement that is most true for you.

My current salary is

❏ Below the low range found in my research

❏ In the low range found in my research

❏ In the middle range found in my research

❏ In the upper range found in my research

❏ Above the upper range found in my research

Based on my experience and ability to deliver a strong ROI, I categorize myself in this level for my promotion position:

❏ The low range found in my research

❏ The middle range found in my research

❏ The upper range found in my research

The difference between my current position and my promotion position is _____

(continued)

(continued)

This represents a _____ percent increase. (To calculate the percentage increase, divide the promotion position figure by the current position salary. For example, if $92,000 is your promotion position figure and $85,000 is your current salary, divide $92,000 by $85,000. This equals 1.08 percent, or an 8 percent increase in salary.)

After calculating this information, develop your target raise in these ranges:

- **Your "reality" number:** The lowest increase you will accept; the bottom line you need to maintain your dignity and work toward your financial and lifestyle goals.

  _____

  _____

- **Your "comfort" number:** An amount you can accept and feel that you are being adequately compensated for your value; a reasonable and realistic goal.

  _____

  _____

- **Your "dream" number:** Your ideal raise and/or the level of compensation commanded by top performers in your target positions.

  _____

  _____

The higher your value to the employer, the more likely you will be able to achieve your "dream" number. What can you do to move yourself up the value chain? Is there a specific skill or expertise that would make you a more desirable candidate? How can you make the case that you are a "star performer" and therefore worthy of higher compensation? Remember, it's not about what you want, need, or deserve (in other words, how long you've been paying your dues); it's all about value.

Step 4: Ask at the Right Time

Recall from chapter 4 that it's important to touch briefly on salary sooner rather than later, so that it doesn't appear you're volunteering to take on more responsibility without getting paid more. Revisit the section "Borrow Language from Sample Conversations" in chapter 4 if needed to refresh your memory on how to bring up salary initially.

When do you return to the subject of salary? After your manager and you have come to agreement on your new role and responsibilities:

> Mr. Manager, I appreciate the opportunity to take on this role formally. Now that we're finalizing the details, I'd like to return to the initial discussions we had around salary.

There's also a wrong time to ask for a raise. Never ask when

- **You can't make ends meet.** Your salary should always be about your contributing value to the company, not the status of your checking account.

- **You've been doing the job for a while.** A cost-of-living increase may be in order, but a raise is not in order for simply doing the job you've been hired to do.

- **You're angry, frustrated, or jealous that someone else on your team got a raise.** Your feelings may be justified, but showing negative emotions, begging, or whining at work only backfires. Vent with a friend (preferably one who is objective, discreet, and employed elsewhere); then strategize and approach your manager calm, cool, and collected.

- **You've recently been given a raise.** Time your request so it's within the norm of company policy. Asking for a raise shortly after just receiving one may call into question your judgment and planning skills.

Step 5: Ask the Right Person(s)

Get the right people in the room for the salary discussion. If your manager doesn't have final authority on your raise, request that whoever does join you. You don't want to offend your manager, but you do want to be sure that matters are resolved with a minimum of back-and-forth discussion. Try phrasing it as a convenience. For example:

> Mr. Manager, I'd like to be present to support you as you bring Ms. Boss up to date on these changes in my role and compensation. To keep it as convenient as possible, may we include Ms. Boss in our discussions?

Or, a more direct request:

> What would it take to get Ms. Boss to join us?

If your manager says,

> Oh, that's alright, no need for you to be there. I'll handle her myself.

Smile and warmly say:

> I've no doubt you can! As you might imagine, this is important to me and I'd really like to be present.

If you can't get the real decision-maker in the room with you, provide your manager with all the ammunition he needs to present your case.

> **Tip:** *Many times, your manager is watching closely to see how well you negotiate salary as a clue to how well you will do at the next level. If you are a pushover when it comes to salary, your manager may think you will be a pushover with your direct reports or customers.*

Step 6: Collaboratively Discuss, Don't Threaten

Practice your negotiations with your coach or mentor to be sure you are coming across with warmth and professionalism. Avoid a tone of voice or body language that might be perceived as demanding or threatening to quit. The language you choose will help. Note the differences in this before-and-after example:

Before:

> Mr. Manager, I expect a $5,000 increase to go with my new role or I just won't be able to stay here.

After:

> Mr. Manager, salary research shows that a role with these responsibilities is paying in the mid-forties on the low end and in the low-fifties on the high end. What kind of results would the company need to see from me to warrant an increase to $52,000?

Note the reference to "What kind of results would the company need" in the preceding example instead of "What kind of results would you need." This language keeps the conversation from becoming a tug of war between you and the manager.

Step 7: Find Common Ground

In successful negotiations, both you and your employer will feel that you've done well and accomplished something. If you walk out of the negotiations having managed to double your work load without getting a salary increase, I guarantee you won't feel good. Likewise, your manager doesn't want to raise your salary without getting good value for the increase.

Common ground acknowledges what both parties want:

> Mr. Manager, I'm really looking forward to this new role and the opportunity to contribute even more value to the company. Let's see if together we can come to an agreement on compensation that is fair and pleases both of us. I've got some salary survey data here, along with the projected ROI we're looking at as I implement this new project. You've also made it clear that the most important results are to bring staff up to speed on current standards and pass the upcoming accreditation.

If your manager's mindset is, "How little can we get away with paying our employees," then just say, "Let's see if together we can come to an agreement on compensation that is fair and equitable" and omit the phrase, "and pleases both of us."

Language to Avoid

Keep in mind that your employer is not really interested in what you want, need, or deserve; their fundamental concern is "What can you do for me?" Therefore, steer clear of language that communicates your wants or needs or expresses any sense of entitlement.

"Before" You-Centered Language	"After" Employer-Centered Language
I really need more.	I'm extremely interested, but I must confess I'm disappointed in the salary increase. Fair market value indicates 15 percent more for a position with this level of responsibility and 25 percent more for someone with my ability to contribute. What flexibility do you have?
Are you sure you can't do more?	How might the position be modified or upgraded to warrant more?

(continued)

(continued)

I can't make a move for less than *X*.	While salary is not my only concern, it is important. I'm eager to contribute and confident of my ability to do so. How can we structure the compensation so that I'm rewarded for meeting established goals?

Step 8: Ask for What You Need

You've heard it said, "You've got nothing to lose by asking." Technically, that's not true. Your manager may become angry or retaliate in some way if he is not a mature manager or the even-keeled type. (Use intuition and good judgment about approaching a volatile manager. And be prepared with how you would respond to the worst-case scenario.) Presuming you've followed the prior steps of setting expectations early in the game and using a collaborative style, you are set to have a calm, reasonable discussion.

Hesitant to Ask for What You Need?

What, if anything, is holding you back from asking for what you need? Limiting beliefs that may be blocking you from asking include the following:

- **Fear of personal rejection:** Ask yourself, "What's the worst that can happen?" And if that happens, what options do you have for a response?

- **Fear of offending or angering your listener:** You have a right to ask for what you need. If your request is framed in a manner that shows benefit to the organization and your listener does become offended or angry, then he is either being irrational or has been caught at the wrong time.

- **Fear of appearing selfish or losing trust:** Again, focus on presenting your request in light of the ROI to your manager and the organization.

- **Fear that you won't get what you want:** This is probably not fear, but disappointment. You may get some of what you want, but not all (at least immediately). If this is the case, get clear with your manager on what his performance expectations are to consider you for the level of position you want.

You've also heard it said of negotiations that "he who blinks [or speaks] first loses." This is not necessarily the case when it comes to negotiating a raise. That's because you already have an idea of the company's pay ranges. The company is apt to be tight-fisted because you're on board as an employee—it's more likely you'll stay with the company than bail,

> **Tip:** *Ask for 20 percent more than you want. This allows room for your manager to negotiate down and feel that she's also won.*

and they know it. Therefore, they're less likely to offer you a big raise. If you ask first, and ask for the maximum (knowing you're willing to compromise), it puts you in the driver's seat. Here's how it might sound:

> From my research, I understand that *X* is the standard for this type of position, which seems fair given my track record of delivering 18 percent ROI.

Note that *X* (above) may be substantially higher than your current salary. Here's another option:

> Again, I'm pleased to have the opportunity to take on this role formally. We've agreed on the position description, your project priorities, and the reporting relationship. Based on this and the research I've done on comparable salaries, I had a figure in mind of *X*, which appears fair given my experience and ability to deliver the results the Board is looking for.

Step 9: Anticipate Objections

Of course, there's the possibility that your salary negotiations will go smoothly:

> Mr. Manager, I'd like a 20 percent increase in salary with this new role.

> Well, Jane, that sounds just great. You're worth every penny, and more! We'll make that happen retroactive to the beginning of the year.

In your dreams!

Instead, expect to encounter objections. In the remainder of this chapter, sales coach Pat Schuler of www.GeminiPro.com offers insightful advice for the most common types of salary objections.

There's Not Enough Money in the Budget

"Many people think the budget discussion comes last," says Schuler. "In reality, it comes very early in the process." For instance:

Mr. Manager, if I'm able to demonstrate that I can contribute to the bottom line, what kind of budget is available to reward that performance?

If the manager says there's nothing available, ask when there might be money:

I respect that reality, Mr. Manager. When does budget money become available. January, you say? I'd be glad to visit the subject now and, provided you see value here, take on my new responsibilities in January.

We Just Don't Do Salary Increases Like That

This objection is a variation on "there's not enough money in the budget." Schuler explains that, "Nine times out of ten, what the employer is really saying is 'you're not bringing in enough value.'"

Schuler recommends countering this objection with a request:

Mr. Manager, what would you need to see from me in order to help you find the budget money? What kind of response, what kind of ROI, what kind of accomplishments would help break that money loose?

You're Already at the Top of the Pay Scale

You may have been at the top of your pay range for your current position, but you're talking about a new set of responsibilities now. You can either address this objection by asking a question:

What would it take to change that?

Or pointing out the facts:

Yes, I understand I was at the top of the pay range in my last position and am proud to have earned that based on performance. As we look at the new situation, the level of responsibility, and the deliverables at hand, this puts me into a new pay range. To be equitable and on par with the industry standard, I understand that X is fair market value for this type of work.

You Can't Receive That Large an Increase in Salary So Soon

For this objection, stay focused on the value you bring to the table and the fair market value for the position.

I understand your concern, Mr. Manager. Based on the research I've done on comparable salaries and the impact this position has on the organization, a competitive salary would be X.

Step 10: Keep the Door Open

Don't give up if you don't get the raise you request. Consider countering with options, such as these:

- Bonus based on production

- Additional vacation time

- Flex-time or telecommuting arrangement

- Wellness programs or gym membership

- Professional association dues

- Membership in community organizations or country clubs for the purposes of networking

- Coaching

- Reimbursement for education and professional development programs

- Stock options

- Gas cards

- Paid time off to volunteer

- Additional staff or interns to support you (or give you management experience if this is an area for development)

- Additional resources for a project you're working on

> **Tip:** Avoid giving your employer the impression that your salary research has led you to the conclusion that you're ready to find greener pastures. This can sound like an ultimatum and alienate your manager.

> **Tip:** Know what you want! In a 2007 CNNMoney.com online poll, when asked whether an extra week's vacation or an extra week's pay would be preferred, more than 8,000 respondents (56 percent) chose more vacation. What's your choice?

If your raise doesn't come through because your manager doesn't perceive he's getting value for the dollars, ask how you can continually improve yourself to qualify for the salary you desire:

Thank you, Mr. Manager. I'm committed to this process. What training, projects, or experiences are available that would provide the development needed?

And, keep the door open for a discussion at an agreed-on date in the future.

> Thank you, Mr. Manager. I'll be working on those skills you've outlined and would like your feedback on where I stand. May we revisit this in six months?

Tip: *As much as possible, remove subjectivity from performance compensation by linking performance bonuses to some provable formula, such as sales volume, profitability, and productivity.*

Remember, the future belongs to those who ask and act!

Key Points: Chapter 6

- Memorize the mantra—"it's all about value." Link salary to performance, never an inability to pay your bills.

- Know the market. Research the going rate for your target position.

- Know what you want. Paint a picture of the best-case scenario and what that would mean to your life. In addition, identify the bottom-line scenario and decide whether you are willing to live with it.

- Ask at the right time. Mention salary early in your promotion discussions and follow up when your new responsibilities have been clarified.

- Ask the right person. Make sure the person(s) with the authority to grant an increase is in the room and engaged in the discussion.

- Collaboratively discuss, don't threaten. Keep the conversation a two-way discussion, not a one-sided ultimatum.

- Find common ground. Be sure your employer will also be getting what they want in this agreement. Your presentation should be rooted in facts.

- Ask for what you want. Make a brief reference to salary early in discussions with your manager. After your new responsibilities are determined, discuss salary in more detail.

- Anticipate objections. Expect them. Learn to overcome them.

- Keep the door open. If all else fails, negotiate for items other than cold hard cash and leave the door open for future discussions.

Chapter 7

Real-Life Success Stories

There's nothing like success stories to inspire hope that you, too, can be promoted. In this chapter you'll read about individuals who, with the help of career coaches and career counselors, built and executed promotion plans that overcame challenging circumstances.

Certified Career Management Coaches (CCMC) from Career Coach Academy (www.CareerCoachAcademy.com) and members of Career Masters Institute (www.cminstitute.com) contributed to the success stories found in this chapter. Their clients' stories are listed alphabetically by the career coach's or counselor's last name. Please feel free to contact them if you need additional help with your promotion plan. Their contact information is in appendix F.

Success Story 1: 32-Year Veteran of One Employer Finally Wins Seat at the Executive Table

Contributed by Barb Poole, B.S., CCMC, CPRW, CERW

Situation

"Jack" is a 51-year-old risk management executive who has worked for the same company for 32 years. During his tenure, his employer has remained a privately held, family-owned corporation and has evolved from a regional to a global operation, with 3,500 employees in both the U.S. and Canada.

Jack started with the company as a laborer while in college. Throughout numerous corporate reorganizations (he has reported to more than 18 CFOs!), he was consistently given increased responsibilities, including quality, contract administration, and most notably, from 1980 to 2003, financial services management. In 2003, the CFO at that time asked Jack to also lead risk management activities, while keeping the title of Financial Services Manager/Assistant Treasurer. In 2004, he was given the official title of Director of Corporate Risk Management. Finance was delegated to another manager. In 2006, at the request of the CEO and Company Owner/Board

Chair, Jack stepped in to turn around an unacceptably high level of financial services delinquencies while continuing in risk management.

Jack contacted me for coaching services because he was, in his words, "an emotional wreck." Despite the fact that he worked 11- to 15-hour days, he loved what he did. However, he felt underappreciated in terms of salary and, most importantly to him, not being included as part of the five-member senior executive team. This was the promotion Jack wanted—admission to this team, with his current position and title and a higher salary. Jack and I worked together over a three-month period, and Jack was able to achieve all his goals within just six weeks.

Client's Challenges

- Was hesitant to bring up the subject of promotion to the boss.
- Faced limited opportunities for promotion within the organization, which is often common in a family-owned company.
- Was not perceived by executives as a logical choice for promotion.
- Was hampered by a strained relationship with his boss.
- Was previously turned down for a promotion.
- Was limited by his style of communicating.
- Lacked a physical appearance in line with members of the senior-level executive team.
- Had gotten lost in the myriad corporate restructurings over a long period of time.
- Was consistently told how much he was valued by the CEO, the Owner/Board Chair, and the top team, but was passed over for promotion and admission to the senior-level executive team.

Strategy

- Used a variety of brainstorming exercises and assessment tools with Jack, and coached him to clarify his needs and wants with his current employer.
- Targeted three core needs that Jack felt were not being met with his employer: income, sense of belonging, and respect.

- Clarified through coaching that Jack was passionate about what he did in his dual roles as Director of Corporate Risk Management and Director of Financial Services.

- Identified that unhappiness and stress were directly correlated to Jack not being paid what he thought he was worth and not being accepted to the core team where he felt he already was a "spoke in the wheel."

- Coached Jack on specific methods to conduct research regarding salary ranges and expectations for people in roles similar to his in comparable organizations, markets, and geographic locations. His salary and level within the organizational chart were both lower than the norm.

- Reviewed with Jack the corporate history/culture and his path within the organization. Clarified the organizational hierarchy changes, out-sourced consultant recommendations, and rapid corporate growth that had resulted in Jack's senior-executive role and its relative components that were or were not in sync with what Jack wanted.

- Championed Jack as he tackled his fears regarding whether he would be invited to join the executive team. In coaching, he addressed how fear was getting in the way of what he wanted, and he identified techniques that empowered and helped him master and control these fears.

- Boosted Jack's self-esteem, giving him the confidence to ask for what he wanted and deserved.

- Captured Jack's value on paper by writing and cataloguing 25 SMART Stories™ to convey his value relative to his employer's motivation to buy.

- Collaborated with Jack to illuminate his career brand, emphasizing three key elements of his value as a corporate liaison, negotiator, and watchdog.

- Developed a three-point marketing message, a verbal business card, and a mini-bio, which were integrated into a five-page branding document explaining in detail why any employer would value his abilities. Each statement was supported by detailed successes.

- Created a resume that clearly conveyed his current status (Senior-Executive, Corporate Risk Management/Financial Services); his branding statement with supporting bullet points; an extensive, centered list of competencies; a career overview; specific successes in both a Challenge-Action-Result (CAR) and a keyword-focused format; current, relevant certifications (to offset his lack of a degree); and an extensive list of professional and community leadership roles, including quantifiable achievements.

- Coached Jack on updating his wardrobe to convey a more professional, polished image consistent with his new executive brand. He acknowledged that the senior executive team wore three-piece suits and ties, while he had not. He purchased several "power" suits, ties, and dress shoes. He started wearing these to work and when asked the reason for the change, he said, "I like to dress like I feel—on top of the world!"

- Identified an extensive list of Jack's many champions, comprising customers, a partner, colleagues, senior executives, and "movers/shakers" in the U.S., Canada, Europe, and Asia. Wrote phone scripts and letter and e-mail templates Jack could use to network and ask people for their testimonials.

- Coached Jack to build a presentation folder that he duplicated to share with the CEO and Owner/Board Chair. This "brag book" was organized and tabulated, containing his branding document; resume; testimonials; letters of recommendation; letters from customers and colleagues regarding specific projects; current leadership credentials and certificates to offset his lack of a degree; impressive executive, leadership-level successes conveyed with newspaper and magazine clippings; graphs showing bottom-line results; and more.

- Coached Jack to avoid negative references to past or current situations, and instead focus on his past, current, and future value. This new "languaging" included references to historical and present successes, as well as possibility-oriented ideas for the future.

- Assisted Jack in writing a formal proposal and coached him in creating an action plan centered on a face-to-face meeting with the CEO and Owner/Board Chair. Included a "Plan B" in case Jack did not hear the answer he wanted.

Results

Jack requested and scheduled a meeting with the CEO and Owner/Board Chair in mid-June.

During the three months of our coaching relationship, Jack experienced an increasing uneasiness because his direct supervisor, the CFO (one of the members of the senior executive team), wanted to take away his Financial Services role out of concern that Jack had "too much on his plate." This would have weakened Jack's position and diminished his brand image.

We created a strategic plan for Jack that bought him some precious and much-needed time. He asked his boss to allow him to demonstrate his ability to handle, and excel in, the dual roles. His boss consented to wait until mid-August to revisit the issue.

When Jack met with the CEO and Owner/Board Chair, as planned, he began by subtly thanking them for taking time to meet with him and allowing him the chance to grow with the organization through the years. This created a subliminal message that he was about to resign in a setting where it would be a corporate hardship to fill his multifaceted roles that were so heavily based on relationships forged with people at all levels, across the globe. Instead, Jack proposed that he be given a "trial" six months to become part of the senior executive team, reporting to the CEO instead of the CFO. During this time, he made it clear that he would *not* expect a raise or any perks enjoyed by the rest of the team. He and the CEO also agreed to meet for 30 minutes a week so that Jack could update him on his progress—a process already in place for the other executive team members.

Within six months, the decision could be made whether to permanently welcome Jack to the team. At that time, he would receive a salary raise comparable to the national average, as well as the perks already offered to the current team. No reference was made as to what might happen if Jack were not made part of the team. (Jack had a plan to move forward with an external job search; however, it was put in storage to be used only if needed.) The CEO and Owner/Board Chair agreed to Jack's proposal.

Long before "D-Day," only six weeks later, the CEO and the Owner/Board Chair called Jack to a three-way meeting and offered him a seat on the senior-executive team as Vice President of Corporate Risk Management, with very specific financial accountability. The position brought with it a substantial raise, company car, new office, expense account, and more. Jack's situation truly reinforces the adage, "If you want the job, ask for it!"

Success Story 2: Employee Earns Nod to Manage His Own Agency

Contributed by Clay Cerny, Ph.D.

Situation

"Edward" is an African-American in his late thirties who worked as an account representative for several years. He joined a leading national insurance company with the dream of one day managing his own agency and being compensated according to his skill and effort, not a commission system.

His initial attempt to make his dream happen was unsuccessful. Edward lost his first bid at managing his own agency because he did not prepare for a thorough, structured panel interview in which a committee of seven experienced agency managers evaluated him. The interview covered seven subject areas, and Edward was not allowed to use any kind of notes except for a concluding statement. Following the interview, the committee told Edward that his presentation didn't demonstrate sufficient knowledge of the company. In addition, he didn't project enough confidence in his ability.

Six months later, he faced the committee again after working with me as his coach over a two-week period that included four sessions, and this time the result of his interview was positive.

Client's Challenges

- Considered too new to the company to be promoted.
- Faced limited opportunities/positions for promotions within the organization.
- Was not well known by the "right" people within the organization.
- Had previously been turned down for the position.
- Lacked the necessary communication skills, both verbal and nonverbal.
- Needed a boost in his confidence.

Strategy

- Identified the required areas of competence that would be covered in the panel interview.

- Formulated talking-points to address each area in a conversational manner.

- Role-played the 45-minute interview, giving equal time to each area that would be covered, along with time for follow-up questions.

- Practiced answers with Edward to ensure that they matched well with the allotted time for each question (five to seven minutes).

- Addressed poor nonverbal communication skills: weak eye contact and keeping arms and hands folded in a way that indicated nervousness.

- Resolved confidence issues that resulted in freezing during answers. Practiced verbal techniques that allowed Edward's responses to sound fluid and professional.

- Developed opening and closing stories to let the committee feel Edward's enthusiasm and commitment.

- Emphasized Edward's recent work with a 20-year veteran of the company, someone he looked to as a coach and mentor.

- Rephrased questions so that Edward would react in a natural manner and not be surprised by a different kind of wording.

- Repeated the practice interview over four sessions until Edward said he was confident and ready to face the committee.

- Planned post-interview strategy (thank-you note, follow-up).

Results

Edward called me the day after the interview to inform me that he had been selected to manage his own agency. He felt that the story we conceived for the conclusion—comparing his business model to a country doctor's office—really won over the committee. He also said that they were impressed by his work with the veteran agent. Playing up this relationship gave him credibility he did not have the first time he met the committee. Edward opened his agency in November. Like most managers in his company, he is likely to stay with the organization for several years, growing a successful business, serving his clients, and living his dream.

Success Story 3: Twenty-Something Makes Rapid Career Progress with Pop Culture and Media Leader

Contributed by Jane Cranston

Situation

"Jenna" was in her mid-twenties when she started working with her coach to transition from a job—a support role for a financial services company—to a career in her area of passion, the field of pop culture and media. Her story includes a move to a new company initially and then rapid advancement within that organization.

Client's Challenges

- Did not major in media in college and had no network to speak of.

- Had no experience or education on how to look for a job that would become a career.

- Stronger analytical skills than management abilities, yet to advance she had to manage people as well as projects.

Strategy

- Coached Jenna to decide and commit to making a move. She then identified potential target companies, who she knew, who she didn't know but would like to, and entry points.

- Landed first job as junior analyst—not her ultimate goal, but a foot in the door with a global media company.

- Worked with Jenna on a three-times-per-month basis to set goals and objectives, establish benchmarks, evaluate progress, strategize before acting in difficult situations, manage her boss, and establish a professional appearance, approach, and communication style.

- Encouraged her to take advantage of career assessments and career development courses offered through the company and always carve out personal time so as not to take away from her productivity time.

- Recommended that Jenna consciously choose to dress at a level that was above her analyst status.

- Coached her to create a brand that focused on high quality—in her projects, she was intentional about doing things only once and with exceptional quality. Jenna always went beyond what her manager and others expected of her with respect to the level of analysis she provided.

- Encouraged Jenna to look for every opportunity to get her signature on reports and projects she was associated with. Or, if that was not possible, write analysis in such a way that it was clear she was the author. Jenna also attended meetings and offered insights at appropriate moments so that it was clear that she was savvy about the business.

- Coached Jenna to request one-on-one meetings every six months with her manager and her manager's boss to create a career plan and timetable. During these meetings, Jenna learned their stories and obtained career advice. She'd also make it clear how she wanted to grow with the company, in what position, and at what salary. She would ask, "What do you see as the obstacles I can either avoid or hurdle?" and "What experiences, skills, and deliverables do I need to move to this next position?" She would obtain buy-in from her managers (not promises) that if she did so, this would happen.

- Consulted Jenna on "work-arounds." For example, in targeting the title of manager but not having anyone to supervise, she asked for an intern, knowing it would give her valuable experience in supervising someone even though managing others was not her favorite task.

- Encouraged her to develop savvy relationships with her manager. For example, she asked her manager where he wanted to be in his career and, knowing his promotion goals, she said, "You want to get promoted and I want to get promoted—how can I help you get promoted so that I can, too?"

- Coached Jenna to become the go-to expert in two media categories. In doing so, she was invited to management meetings that weren't normally attended by employees at her level. This gave her exposure to high-level executives across division lines. Because of the time it took to develop her new expertise, she would often work nights to continue to shine in her business analyst responsibilities.

- Coached Jenna to increase her visibility. In order to be seen by executives in a functional area she was targeting, she looked for opportunities to change her traffic patterns and be in other parts of the building where these individuals worked.

- Worked with Jenna on advocating for her goals during performance reviews. When salary was discussed at the end of the review and a raise offered that was below her goal, Jenna learned to name her number saying, "Thank you very much but my goal is to be at $75,000 by December of this year. What would need to occur to make that happen?" She made it clear that, in addition to the responsibilities and authority, title and money was important to her—she was looking at the whole package.

- Coached Jenna through her decision to accept a lateral move in the firm at one point to gain more experience.

Results

Within a few months of signing on with the organization, Jenna was promoted from junior analyst to analyst, and in less than one year was promoted to manager. She went on to hold positions as Senior Analyst and Analyst—Special Projects. Jenna branded herself as an expert in a specific customer category. Because of this, she was invited to present at high-level internal meetings and was chosen to represent her organization at national conferences on her area of expertise. This activity also put her on the radar screen of competitors, increasing her awareness of her marketability and boosting her confidence regarding other career opportunities.

Success Story 4: Independent Consultant Doubles Income in One Month

Contributed by George Dutch, CCM, CMF, JCTC

Situation

"Gordon" works as an independent consultant providing benefits packages to clients on behalf of insurance companies. When he first contacted me, he was developing an unrelated "workshops business" and wanted to double his then-current income from his benefits consulting work from $2,000 to $4,000 a month, giving him enough time and financial freedom to invest in, grow, and nurture his new business.

We identified and reviewed several options that might allow Gordon to achieve his goals, and we determined that his most likely chance to boost his revenue to the desired level was to contact companies for which he had previously consulted and that were already familiar with the quality of his work.

Subsequently, Gordon contacted and arranged a meeting with an employee-benefits company based in another city that he had previously contracted with and that had offered him a full-time position the preceding year. Gordon met with the company as planned, and they offered him an opportunity to work for them on a contract basis, servicing a large ongoing client who needed to work with someone local, which Gordon was, five to ten days per month.

When the subject of compensation arose, Gordon requested to be paid a rate of $350 per diem—the same rate he had billed this company when he worked for them in the preceding year. The company, however, countered his request and offered to pay him $45 per hour for his work on the account, figuring that the account would require five to seven hours of Gordon's time per month. In addition to this, the company proposed a co-brokered arrangement with Gordon that would make him a select broker and put him in direct competition with about 15 other brokers in his hometown.

Gordon was dismayed by the company's offer and very disappointed that it didn't even come close to matching what he expected. If the company agreed to his terms, he would earn an additional $1,750 to $3,500 per month, which would make his financial goals viable and allow him plenty of time to devote to his workshops business. Instead, the $45-per-hour pay the company proposed was about one-third of the $132-per-hour rate he typically billed his own accounts and represented only $270 per month in ongoing revenue, compared to the $350 per diem he had billed the same company just one year previously.

The situation was further complicated by the fact that Gordon was strongly averse to working as a select broker. The mechanics of doing business in that manner did not suit Gordon's style. He preferred to work on a few accounts and "go deep"—really get to know the client and their business goals and match the benefits packages accordingly. The co-brokerage arrangement required the opposite; he would be pulled in different directions by many sources.

When Gordon initially considered the company's counteroffer, he felt his best option was to pass on it.

Client's Challenges

- Lacked a winning style of communicating.
- Wanted to double his current income to $4,000 per month.
- Needed a boost in his self-confidence.

Strategy

- Coached Gordon to not take personally the first offer presented by the employee benefits company and allowed him to vent his disappointment.
- Encouraged Gordon to separate his feelings from the business transaction.
- Asked Gordon questions to help him identify and focus on what was most important to him.
- Assisted Gordon in crafting a professional e-mail reply to the employee benefits company that projected both clarity and confidence.

Results

Gordon became clearer about what was important to him and more confident that what he wanted was possible. Gordon submitted his counteroffer and the general manager of the employee benefits company accepted it within the month.

That same month, Gordon achieved his financial target of doubling his income to $4,000. He was very happy with this accomplishment because the additional revenue allowed him to pay his bills without working full-time hours, and perhaps best of all, this arrangement allowed him the time and energy to be more personally proactive in developing his workshops business, giving him a greater sense of personal fulfillment and peace.

Success Story 5: Account Manager's Initiative Fast-Forwards Her Promotion to Associate Director

Contributed by Dale Kurow, M.S.

Situation

"Emmeline" is a senior account manager with an interactive company in New York City. She had been told by the company that she might be up for promotion to associate director but was also told she had some areas to improve on. A year had gone by with no change in her status. Emmeline wanted to know what steps she could take to help her get the promotion she felt she deserved.

Client's Challenges

- Needed to improve her communication and presentation skills.

- Was not approaching projects with a global organizational perspective.

Strategy

- Coached Emmeline to connect with her industry colleagues and research www.salary.com for comparable salary data.

- Prepared documentation supporting her growth, including an updated resume and an accomplishments summary with specific improvements about her skill.

- Assisted Emmeline to enhance her communication and presentation skills. For example, introduced simple communication tips, such as being cognizant to pause and breathe intentionally during presentations, lowering her voice, working from 3 × 5–inch cue cards, checking in by asking, "Are there any questions so far?" and finding a friendly face in the audience to focus on when she felt nervous.

- Advised Emmeline on improving her global perspective by developing an overall strategy before presenting specific ideas. For instance, she began asking herself questions such as, "How does the suggestion I'm thinking of making impact the company as a whole?" or "What research has the company already done that would add to my knowledge of this situation?"

- Worked with her to compose or edit important e-mails, including one requesting a review meeting with her manager with words to this effect: "As you know, some time ago we talked about the fact that I might be eligible for promotion. I'd like to discuss this with you at your convenience and look forward to sharing some of the forward progress that's been made in this regard."

- Helped her thoroughly prepare for her review meeting with an internal resume and accomplishments, as well as revenues generated as a result of her ideas. In addition, helped her rehearse improvements in the areas of communications/presentations and global perspective.

- Collaborated with Emmeline to develop a Plan B in case the promotion didn't come through so that she felt as though she had a full, well-rounded plan.

Results

In a few short months, Emmeline won her promotion to associate director. She conveyed that she reached goals she never thought she could reach at her job. Her confidence increased as she overcame obstacles that she initially wasn't even aware of. The employer was very receptive to Emmeline's presentation at the review meeting and commented that they would have "gotten around to promoting her," but her initiative persuaded them to move faster.

Success Story 6: Financial Services Executive Lands Officer-Level Opportunity After Long Delay

Contributed by Bobbie LaPorte, MBA

Situation

"Laura" is a female executive in her early forties, working for an international, Fortune 100 financial services firm. She has been at this organization for more than eight years, primarily in client services and product development roles; previously she served in similar roles in a smaller organization.

When we started working together she was serving in a critical, high-visibility liaison role between the organization's product and IT business units. Because of this and previous assignments, she possessed a very specialized knowledge base about the company's business. Through multiple organizational and direct supervisory changes, Laura had "survived" in the organization, but her superiors felt she had some serious liabilities in the areas of building critical internal relationships, acting in a more "strategic" manner in her role, and communicating in a more professional manner. She had been given feedback to this effect over the last two-plus years, but had also been told her promotion to Vice President (officer-level) was imminent.

Laura felt that she had been doing the same level of work as her peers—many of whom had been promoted earlier—and that she was being unfairly passed over for promotion. Her goal was to gain the respect and recognition for her work and contributions—the title was most important to her, whereas the associated compensation and continued upward mobility was of lesser importance.

With a new organizational change and supervisor, she was offered the opportunity to hire a coach to help her address areas for growth and demonstrate her readiness for a promotion. We began working together in June.

Client's Challenges

- Had been given additional responsibilities in the past without receiving a salary increase.

- Was not known or well known by the "key" people within the company.

- Had a peer in her department with a VP title who was routinely taking credit for her ideas and accomplishments.

- Received a negative 360-degree evaluation.

- Lacked a global perspective of the organization.

- Had a communication style that was less than ideal.

Strategy

- Worked with Laura to clarify her career goals and motivations—short-term, VP promotion; and long-term, options outside of current employer.

- Reviewed comprehensive 360-degree interviews to identify skills, qualifications, and personal development needs for Laura to improve on in order to ensure her success in a new role.

- Created a 90-day development plan to address gaps—including internal management development, training programs, and active coaching.

- Defined key peer and management relationships that Laura could establish and that were collaborative and supportive of a VP promotion.

- Coached Laura on improving her communication style to be more collaborative and inclusive.

- Identified projects and initiatives that could provide Laura with the visibility and strategic content to demonstrate her capabilities and value.

- Actively coached Laura on opportunities to contribute on more strategic levels in meetings, take ownership of projects, and demonstrate confidence in decisions and actions.

- Coached Laura on taking the initiative to provide weekly updates to management on plans (to demonstrate and showcase progress)—particularly around projects that her peer manager would often take responsibility and credit for; spent additional time coaching Laura on how to proactively address this issue with her peer as well.

- Assisted with the definition and development of an operating plan for Laura's unit, including a staffing plan, and support of skills and knowledge transfer to staff.

- Continually challenged Laura to give up tactical work to staff, and to define and delegate developmental responsibilities for staff going forward.

- Challenged client to set boundaries around checking voice mail and e-mail after hours and to identify one outside interest/activity that she could pursue at least one day a week.

Results

Laura was placed on the promotion list within a few months of working together and formally promoted to Vice President in less than six months.

She responded well to the feedback and coaching and accepted that "perception is everything." She realized that it didn't matter how she saw herself and her capabilities if the powers that be saw her differently. She was able to temper and improve her communications style, develop a strong team of professionals, and build an effective operating unit. Follow-up interviews indicated that she was being seen in a more positive light by peers and senior management, was acting with confidence, and had successfully made significant contributions to business strategy.

Following a recent major organizational change, her direct supervisor was promoted, and she was asked to assume responsibility for his entire organization. She also received the highest possible bonus payout and salary increase at year-end. And for the first time in more than eight years, she did not take her PDA with her on a recent 10-day vacation!

Success Story 7: First-Generation Immigrant Gets Brand Makeover and 43 Percent Raise

Contributed by Sharon McCormick, M.S., MCC, NCCC, NCC, CPRW

Situation

"Anna" is a 35-year-old, first-generation immigrant from Puerto Rico who relocated to the United States to be near family. She works in the human resources department at a global computer solutions company with 90,000+ employees and has been there for five years. She was a recruiter with a salary of $35,000 when she contacted me for help in advancing her career. Anna worked in retail prior to her position and earned a Bachelor's degree in Business. She is bilingual. When we originally began working together, Anna wanted to work in another industry so that she could advance to a management position. At that time, she thought that was the only way she could earn more money.

We worked together for one month, meeting once a week for two hours, when she called to tell me that her company promoted her to a manager position with a salary of $50,000. This was very smart on their part, as Anna is a bright, polished, professional, and ambitious lady who would have been easily hired elsewhere. Now she has the company's undivided loyalty and appreciation, which in turn made her a happier employee and motivational manager to her direct reports.

Client's Challenges

- Anna was hesitant to bring up the subject of promotion to the boss.

- Faced internal politics—there was no real history of promoting someone to a management position who was so "young" and "new" to the company.

- Had been given additional responsibilities in the past without successfully negotiating a salary increase. She had taken on more and more recruiting duties, and even trained new recruiters, for no additional pay.

- Was not known or well known by the "right" people within the organization.

- Was not perceived by supervisors as a logical choice for promotion because she had no real visibility and hadn't showcased her accomplishments and value.

- Had no successor in place and would create a vacuum in the organization if promoted.

- Did not have a global perspective of the organization, especially in the area of networking or soliciting a mentor.

- Had a passive boss who took little interest in her career goals.

- Needed a boost in her confidence.

Strategy

- Supported Anna in gaining confidence and developing a clearer vision that she could exceed her own expectations in her desired industry. Worked with her to develop practical steps she could take to achieve her goals, and held her accountable for implementing agreed-upon steps.

- Used valid and reliable assessments to help her realize her occupational work preferences, work function interests, values, learning style, and interpersonal style.

- Completed an informal 360-degree assessment so that I could incorporate the additional feedback into my overall impressions of her personality and potential. This illuminated Anna's career potential and interests very thoroughly.

- Assigned her the task of getting a mentor at work as an additional way to get advice on her current company's expectations for her function.

- Gave Anna a worksheet to complete that highlighted her "top ten" accomplishments in a specific format. We then reviewed this together and it allowed us to more easily identify her valuable career traits as a consistent "theme or image" emerged. Those traits were then incorporated into her personal brand.

- Provided Anna with resources in a separate industry that she originally wanted to target. Staying at her current company was a backup plan until she could make the switch.

- Helped Anna identify how to approach her boss verbally with her updated information and demonstrate her value and dedication in a more tangible way.

- Rewrote her resume to convey a more polished executive image, and then had her give it to her boss to "update" her information.

- Encouraged her to pursue the function where I thought she would shine at her current company, which truly leveraged the work she had done for them in the past and gave her exposure to a "hot" function for the future.

- Encouraged her to obtain a relevant national certification that would add to her credibility in the hot function. She was very interested in this and followed up immediately. She stated that previously she had no idea about the hot field or the national certification.

- Encouraged her to network and provided information on several relevant professional organizations and local meetings.

- Sent her job leads that she could apply to and called my current HR contacts in her industry to identify more job leads in Anna's desired industry.

Results

After 20 years in the field as a career counselor, even I was surprised when Anna eagerly called to tell me she had been promoted in her own company—just from being more visible and by updating her resume and accomplishments. Our work together helped Anna crystallize her goals, reposition her for her desired industry, and reaffirm her value at the current company.

What really caught the company's attention was her speaking about her future certification and goals in that hot specialty area. The company will need her help in this area in the future, too, so they realized that they wanted to keep her!

Her new executive-level resume helped to change her image in the company's view, repositioning her from an entry-level recruiter to a potential "star" for the company. She was suddenly viewed as the ambitious, results-oriented, stable, future-achiever that she is; and the company responded better than anyone expected, truly exceeding expectations.

Anna is following through on her certification and her networking. I encouraged her to write an article for her industry, which was published. She framed the article and displays it in her new office. She mentioned her mentor in the article, which the mentor appreciated. This turned out to be an incredible win-win for Anna and the company. She is so happy and "loyal for life" to the company.

Success Story 8: College Secretary "Graduates" to Assistant Director

Contributed by Marcia Merrill, M.Ed., M.S., CCMC, JCTC

Situation

"Monica" is in her mid-forties and had worked as a secretary at a liberal arts college for seven years. In that time, she went back to college and earned her Bachelor's degree in Business Administration and was working on her MBA.

When Monica first contacted me she was in the midst of a divorce. Faced with providing for herself financially, armed with a college degree, and sparked with ambition to earn more money and put her business knowledge into practice, Monica was ready for more responsibility and a promotion. This meant stepping out of her secretarial role and into a more challenging position that would make better use of her degree. She wanted to become the Assistant Director of Development at the college.

Client's Challenges
- Was reluctant to bring up the subject of promotion to her boss.
- Had limited opportunities for promotion within the organization.

- Battled internal politics as a secretary who, despite the fact that she was very professional, was not viewed as such. The situation was further complicated by the fact that she was older than the people to whom she reported.

- Had been given additional responsibilities in the past without receiving a pay increase.

- Was not known or well known by the "right" people within the organization.

- Had an Assistant Director who often took credit for her ideas and accomplishments.

- Was not perceived as a logical choice for a promotion.

- Had a passive boss who took little interest in her career goals.

- Needed a boost in her self-confidence and a change in her mindset; believed she was too old to be promoted.

Strategy

- Clarified what Monica truly wanted in her career—to have more impact and responsibility—and evaluated the likelihood of her current employer being able to meet those wants.

- Identified what Monica enjoyed and did not enjoy in her current job.

- Utilized the DiSC assessment as a starting point in comparing Monica's ideal work environment with her current one.

- Coached Monica and helped her realize that she was indeed happy working for her current employer; assisted her in crystallizing her goals for achieving greater satisfaction with her employer in a new job function.

- Brainstormed ways Monica could bring up a "career development" conversation with her boss, and role-played different scenarios until she found one that felt comfortable for her.

- Coached Monica on her fears surrounding the idea of bringing up career development. Through daring to explore worst-case scenarios, Monica discovered that she had an irrational fear that she might be fired for merely bringing up the subject, end up not being able to afford her rent, and wind up homeless. No wonder she was scared to bring up this topic with her boss! This process empowered Monica and helped her release the fear that had been holding her back.

- Encouraged Monica to "own" her achievements by asking her questions about how she had succeeded in the past. This helped boost her self-confidence and realize her ability to make things happen.

Results

Monica and I worked together for six months, and in that time she realized her goals of being promoted, earning more money, and making a more significant impact with her current employer.

When the college created a new Assistant Director position, they immediately hired Monica for the role. Monica was thrilled to leave behind her secretarial role and take on new challenges and responsibilities commensurate with her academic achievements, professional abilities, and the person she wanted to be and was becoming.

Success Story 9: Project Coordinator Breaks Six-Figure Salary Ceiling

Contributed by Judit Price, M.S., CCM, CDFI, IJCTC, CPRW, CCM

Situation

"Pat" works as a project coordinator for a large medical device manufacturer. She is in her late thirties and has been with her current employer for six years. Throughout her tenure, she has retained the same title, although her salary and job responsibilities have grown along with her experience and technical expertise. Pat's starting salary was $55,000, and she is now earning $75,000 annually.

When Pat and I began working together, she felt that to be fairly compensated for her responsibilities and workload, she deserved a six-figure salary. Pat also wanted her employer to give her the title and full responsibilities of a manager.

Pat's position required technical skills, but also more nuanced skills, such as the ability to handle diplomatic negotiations, create a "common vision" within the project community, and resolve myriad operational issues.

Accomplishing these types of tasks proved very challenging for Pat, and when we started working together, she was eager to strengthen these skills so that she could advance her career and realize her income goals.

Client's Challenges

- Was hesitant to bring up the subject of promotion to her boss.

- Felt intimidated by her supervisor and resented that many of her ideas were "stolen."

- Was not known or well known by the "right" people within the organization.

- Was not perceived by supervisors as a logical choice for promotion because she had no real visibility and hadn't showcased her accomplishments and value.

- Had no successor in place and would create a vacuum in the organization if promoted.

- Did not have a global perspective of the organization, especially in the area of networking or soliciting a mentor.

- Had a difficult relationship with her boss.

- Had previously been turned down for a promotion.

- Had a less-than-ideal style of communicating.

- Needed a boost in her self-confidence.

- Conveyed a physical appearance that needed improvement.

Strategy

- Utilized assessments to help Pat understand her strengths and weaknesses, and how they were perceived by others; assessments used included the Reach 360, MBTI, and CISS.

- Coached Pat regarding her areas of strength to build self-esteem, and coached her on areas for development, most notably her style of communicating.

- Collaborated with Pat to create an action plan that addressed developmental areas and helped her discover the empowerment to make necessary improvements.

- Assisted Pat in defining and developing a personal brand that demonstrated her value.

- Challenged Pat to identify projects that would allow her to showcase her talents and demonstrate her commitment to career development. As a result, Pat volunteered for two difficult, high-profile projects and executed each successfully, benefiting the organization and improving the way she was viewed by key people in the company.

Results

Within a six-month period following the completion of our work together, Pat was promoted and given a raise that took her income to the six-figure bracket she wanted and deserved.

By volunteering to take on the two high-profile projects, Pat demonstrated the necessary skills and professionalism needed to buttress a promotion and a salary increase.

By communicating with more sensitivity to others and projecting more confidence in her own abilities, Pat succeeded in changing the perceptions of key people that had previously limited her growth, thereby enhancing her reputation with both peers and management.

Prior to our work together, Pat's technical skills and creativity were generally appreciated. After completing coaching, Pat exhibited true leadership traits. She learned to reach out to peers and turn them into allies; and she discovered the importance of managing herself in order to influence how others perceived her. In the end, Pat was happier than she had ever been before. She earned the job she wanted, at the salary she wanted, and succeeded in navigating the complexities of the organization and developing skills that would benefit her throughout her career.

Success Story 10: Counselor Convinces Company of Promotion to Supervisor with 28 Percent Raise

Contributed by Beth Woodworth, M.S., JCTC, CRPCC, CDFI, CAC, GFMF, CWDP

Situation

"Amy" is in her early thirties and works as a vocational counselor for a small, private nonprofit company that is funded primarily with federal grant money. Amy, who holds a master's degree, earns $27,000 a year and has been with the company about a year assisting job seekers getting off welfare or going through layoffs.

When Amy and I began working together, she was ready to take on more responsibility and make use of supervisory skills and experience she had acquired in previous positions. An ambitious woman, Amy wanted to be promoted to supervisor in the counseling department and receive a $5,000 salary increase. She also wanted to participate in community collaborations and in-house program development.

Client's Challenges

- Was considered too "new" to the company to be promoted. She had worked at the company only one year.

- Faced internal politics, including a situation with people who had been with the company longer who felt they were not being fairly compensated and people who had been there two to six years longer than Amy and wanted the same promotion.

- Hampered by a situation in which another vocational counselor was taking credit for her ideas and accomplishments.

- Received a poor performance evaluation.

- Lacked confidence and needed a boost to her self-esteem.

Strategy

- Clarified what Amy truly wanted at this point in her career and determined that she could obtain it from her current employer.

- Coached Amy to articulate the specific responsibilities she would be required to perform if she received the promotion and had Amy explain in detail how she was capable of meeting the demands of that role. This helped boost Amy's self-confidence and improved her ability to articulate her qualifications for the higher-level position.

- Assisted Amy in polishing and updating her application materials, resume, and cover letter to give Amy a competitive edge, highlight her accomplishments, and reflect her relevant experience (in other words, supervisory responsibilities).

- Challenged Amy to create a portfolio where she could showcase her achievements and demonstrate her value; items included examples of processes Amy had innovated to improve productivity, certificates she had earned, and accomplishments she had documented.

- Worked with Amy to create a proposal that she would present to management outlining future challenges faced by the candidate selected for the promotion, challenges faced by the organization as a whole, and the specific steps she would take to effectively address and meet those challenges head-on.

- Coached Amy regarding people within the organization who would confirm her capabilities for the new role and helped her identify a comfortable way to approach those individuals about using them as references.

- Collaborated with Amy to identify more opportunities to position herself in a lead-worker type of role (in other words, presenting certain topics on team meeting agendas without "stepping on the manager's toes").

- Encouraged Amy to do what was in her control, such as including her name on documents she created to discourage a particular colleague from taking credit for Amy's work.

- Addressed Amy's fashion choices and coached Amy to study the styles of clothing worn by those at the management level she was targeting. In response to this, Amy adjusted her wardrobe to "dress for success."

- Brainstormed strategies for Amy to present to management explaining how she would handle other members of the department who had more seniority than she and who she would be supervising if promoted.

- Clarified the qualities that made Amy stand out above the other candidates; most notable were her organizational skills, interpersonal skills, and conflict-resolution abilities.

- Coached Amy to further demonstrate her value by having her identify numerous ways to save the company money; this involved creating newer, more efficient practices and processes.

- Ensured Amy's success for closing the deal by practicing behavioral interview questions with her and coaching her on winning salary negotiation techniques.

Results

In just three and a half weeks, Amy succeeded in securing a promotion to Senior Career Counselor and a raise that brought her new salary to $32,000.

Amy was very responsive to the various strategies we discussed and did a wonderful job of implementing them—leveraging her previous supervisory experience, enlisting the support of key players in the company, and projecting the confidence and forethought needed to demonstrate her ability to effectively meet the demands of her new position. Amy remains employed by the same company today and is happy in her new role.

Success Story 11: Director Beats Out 347 for Coveted Senior Staff Position

Contributed by Heather Zeng, Ph.D., LPC, NCC, NCCC, MCC

Situation

"Richard" is a male in his mid-fifties who works as a mid-level department director for a regional energy company in the United Kingdom. Richard is an expatriate who worked abroad for several years before marrying a local national and settling into life in the UK.

When Richard learned that the company was diversifying and creating two senior staff positions to lead and develop work teams to meet new initiatives, he was immediately interested in the opportunity. Although Richard found his present work stimulating, he felt stagnant in his position. He was excited about the potential for broader opportunity within the company and felt ready to take on new responsibilities and challenges. If he succeeded in landing one of the prime positions, he would receive a substantial raise—his salary would jump from £45,000 (about $88,000) to £56,000 (about $109,000). In addition, he would be issued a company car, a Jaguar—an attractive perk as fuel and maintenance of cars is particularly expensive in the UK.

Client's Challenges

- Faced intense competition, both internal and external, for the highly coveted jobs due to limited opportunities in that region of the UK.

- Was challenged as an expatriate to assimilate to the culture of the country and the organization.

- Had weaknesses, both verbal and nonverbal, in his style of communicating; was perceived as having a "tough guy" image, despite the fact that he was respected for his work.

- Did not project the polished look of someone in a leadership role in the UK, where people are notoriously discerning regarding fashion choices, including the cut and quality of one's suits.

- Lacked visibility within the organization.

- Was at risk for age discrimination due to a precedent in the company that favored hiring younger employees.

- Needed a boost in his self-confidence.

Strategy

- Coached Richard on important things to emphasize (such as his leadership skills) and avoid (such as his desire for a company car) when interviewing.

- Helped Richard identify three key skill sets, along with specific achievements from his career to support each, that would be assets to his receiving the promotion.

- Role-played behavioral interview scenarios to help Richard improve his comfort level and address leadership and teamwork skills precisely in a Challenge-Action-Result (CAR) format.

- Assigned Richard the task of selecting clothing that projected a more stylish, polished look.

- Encouraged Richard to participate in high-level public relations events to improve his visibility.

- Emboldened Richard to emphasize his direct and indirect work to support multinational teams; challenged Richard to move beyond his comfort zone, if an opportunity presented itself, and take credit for his achievements—particularly difficult for him in a cultural setting that values modesty.

- Coached Richard to be more restrained in his nonverbal gestures to help him appear less intimidating and more self-assured.

- Presented Richard with four formats of action: planning documents he could use in the final round of interviewing; strategies for approaching the fictitious problem he would be evaluated on; a system to help Richard keep things simple to ensure he would finish his work within the allotted timeframe; and action-planning documents—he practiced these with knowledgeable business friends who would be able to provide valuable feedback on his approach and leadership style.

- Coached Richard on methods for quickly assessing and addressing each team member's strengths, regardless of his previous knowledge of them or lack thereof; also encouraged Richard to assign a timekeeper.

Results

Richard and I worked together for eight weeks total. The openings were listed in January, and Richard was offered his position in the beginning of March, beating out 347 other applicants. He was so delighted he sent me a large plant and a thank-you card.

Richard sailed through the first two interview panels using the behavioral-based formula (Challenge-Action-Result or CAR) we practiced during our coaching sessions. His third round of interviewing was likewise a success. The panel evaluating Richard loved the action-planning worksheets he used to approach the scenario. Soon after the third interview, Richard received an invitation to lunch, where the company formally offered him the position and he happily accepted.

Appendix A

Assessments and Tools to Gain a Competitive Edge

R eliable, validated assessments along with informal survey instruments can help you fast-forward your career by providing self-awareness of your strengths (or areas for development), along with your personal brand, work values, communications style, leadership style, and much more. Some tools have already been mentioned in various chapters. For convenience, those along with others with a variety of price points are included here alphabetically (this list is by no means exhaustive). Thanks go to career and leadership coach Kathy Bitschenauer for compiling this information that will be of value in your ongoing career management.

Assessment Name and Where to Access	Cost	Description
The BarOn EQ-i® Available online at www.6seconds.org/xcart/ product.php?productid=97 Also available through Multi-Health Systems, Inc., by e-mailing customerservice@mhs.com or calling (800) 456-3003.	$150+	A social emotional intelligence assessment that measures one's self-reported potential to deal with daily environmental demands and pressures and helps predict success in both professional and personal pursuits. Requires facilitation by a qualified individual, typically a 30-minute debrief with a psychologist or trained professional.
The Birkman Method® Requires working with a Birkman Certified Consultant: www.birkman.com/contact/ locate_consultant.php	Up to $169	Focuses on five domains: productive and stress behaviors, underlying needs, motivations, and organizational orientation. A sample report can be seen here: www.careerlab.com/assessment/birkman.htm
Career Leader Available online at www.careerleader.com (click on "Individual Clients")	$95	A comprehensive assessment tool for business careers. It includes three Web-based inventories: The Business Career Interest Inventory measures eight core functions, the Management and Professional Profile assesses your values about work rewards, and the Management and Professional Abilities Profile provides information about your business skills and strengths.

Assessment Name and Where to Access	Cost	Description
Careerstrength™ Available online at www.notjustapaycheck.com	Free	Based on temperament theory, this assessment identifies whether your skill set, learning style, and self-leadership style matches your career.
Clifton StrengthsFinder Available through purchase of the book, *Now, Discover Your Strengths* (a unique user code is provided with each book)	$30 (list price)	Provides your top 5 out of 34 themes of talent. It is based on a model of Positive Psychology. Books are available at discounts online (www.amazon.com).
Kiersey™ Temperament Sorter®-II (KTS®-II) Available online at www.advisorteam.com	$14.95	Identifies 16 personality type patterns derived from the four temperament variations. Describes your temperament and the four temperaments. Choose the Corporate Temperament Report or Team Temperament Report.
Knowdell Motivated Skills Card Sort Purchase this card deck from www.careertrainer.com (click on the Bookstore and Assessments tab)	$7 (+ shipping)	Self-scoring card sort that identifies your motivated skills, burnout skills, and skills you'd like to develop. Use to easily and quickly assess your proficiency and motivation in 51 transferable skills areas.

(continued)

(continued)

Assessment Name and Where to Access	Cost	Description
Locus of Control Survey Available online at www.dushkin.com/connectext/psy/ch11/survey11.mhtml	Free	Assesses the extent to which you believe internal or external forces are responsible for your success or failure. People with an internal locus of control believe that success is contingent on what they do; those with an external locus of control believe that events outside their personal control determine success.
O*NET® Work Importance Profiler (WIP) Available online at www.onetcenter.org/WIP.html	Free	Provides your top two work values (whether achievement, independence, recognition, relationships, support, or working conditions) and top 10 work needs. Requires downloading software (7M file size); works best with high-speed Internet connection.
Positive Impact Test Available online at http://dipperandbucket.com	Free	Assesses your positive attitude, including suggestions for improvement. After working on your positive attitude, you can take the test again to see your progress.

Assessment Name and Where to Access	Cost	Description
Reach 360 Available online at www.reachcc.com/360reach	$29.97	Personal branding tool that gathers anonymous input from colleagues, coworkers, friends, and others on your brand attributes. A reality check on how others perceive you.
Self Worth Inventory Available online at www.crgleader.com	$13.95	Helpful if you'd like to boost your confidence. Identifies your present level of self-worth and provides guidelines for increasing your self-worth. Printed or online.
Stress Resiliency Profile Available online at www.cpp.com	$12.50	Measures mental habits that determine your level of "stress resiliency." Three cognitive habits that create stress are identified and evaluated: • *Deficiency focusing:* the habit of focusing on the negatives at the expense of the positives • *Necessitating:* the perception that tasks are inflexible demands that must be met • *Low skill recognition:* the tendency to underestimate or not recognize one's own competence and abilities. The profile measures your level of use of each of these habits and shows where stress symptoms are most likely to occur. It offers guidelines to help design a strategy for increasing stress resiliency.

(continued)

(continued)

Assessment Name and Where to Access	Cost	Description
TKI (Thomas-Kilman Conflict Mode Instrument) Available online at www.cpp.com (type TKI in Search box in upper-left corner on Web site, or click on TKI tab on the top menu bar)	$11.75	Measures how you solve interpersonal conflicts (whether two people or a team); it provides the test taker with the five conflict modes, questions to consider for each conflict mode, and appropriate uses of each conflict mode.
Values Preference Indicator Available online at www.crgleader.com	$13.95	Identifies your core values and the needs and fears associated with them. Printed or online assessment.
Work Behavior Inventory Available at www.HRConsultantsInc.com or by e-mailing jenny.schumann@hrconsultantsinc.com	$9.99	Measures 43 scales grouped according to research evidence on the Big Five personality factors. Helpful for focusing career development and coaching efforts on the behaviors that may be most relevant to success, as well as diagnosing natural "blind spots" that may inhibit an individual from reaching their full career potential.

Once you have taken the assessments, discuss the reports with someone familiar with interpreting assessments, such as a career coach or career counselor. Although self-assessments are often quite accurate, the results should be carefully reviewed and validated—you have the final say-so in what is true for you. The exception to this would be a 360° assessment where coworkers or managers anonymously provide feedback on their perceptions of your work and/or leadership style. From the results, you can develop a plan to capitalize on your strengths and shore up any weaknesses or natural blind spots.

Beyond using assessments, be proactive about your professional growth and development. Attend workshops, teleseminars, or courses related to strengths you want to build or gaps to overcome. Read related books, articles, and blogs. Here are some suggested resources for understanding personality type, strengths, and team communications:

- *The EQ Edge* by Steven J. Stein, Ph.D., and Howard E. Book, M.D. (Wiley, 2006)

- *The Five Dysfunctions of a Team* by Patrick M. Lencioni (Jossey-Bass, 2002)

- *Go Put Your Strengths to Work: 6 Powerful Steps to Achieve Outstanding Performance* by Marcus Buckingham (Free Press, 2007)

- *How Full Is Your Bucket?: Positive Strategies for Work and Life* by Tom Rath and Donald O. Clifton, Ph.D. (Gallup Press, 2004)

- *Now, Discover Your Strengths* by Marcus Buckingham and Donald O. Clifton, Ph.D. (Free Press, 2001)

- *Please Understand Me II: Temperament, Character, Intelligence,* by David Kiersey (Prometheus Nemesis Book Company, 1998)

- *Quick Guide to the 16 Personality Types and Teams: Applying Team Essentials™ to Create Effective Teams* by Linda V. Berens, Linda K. Ernst, and Melissa A. Smith (Telos Publications, 2004)

- *StrengthsFinder 2.0: A New and Upgraded Edition of the Online Test from Gallup's Now, Discover Your Strengths* by Tom Rath (Gallup Press, 2007)

- *Understanding Yourself and Others: An Introduction to Temperament* by Linda V. Berens (Telos Publications, 2000)

In addition, many of the assessment sites listed previously offer newsletters and free articles. Check them out.

SMART Story™ Worksheet

Copy this worksheet as needed to write additional SMART Stories™ as described in chapter 4.

SMART STORY™ WORKSHEET

Situation and More:

Your role: _____

_____

When: _____

Who else was involved or impacted: _____

_____

What was the task or challenge? _____

_____

_____

_____

Action:

What was your thought process? What steps did you take? What decisions were made? Describe the sequence. _____

_____

_____

_____

_____

_____

(continued)

(continued)

Results:

Use numbers to relate your results.

_____

_____

_____

Tie-in/Theme:

Competencies: _____

_____

How this story ties to your organization's priorities and goals:

_____

_____

_____

Identify Your Energy, Perception, Judgment, and Orientation Preferences

In the tables that follow, you'll find a self-scoring personality instrument that you can use to gauge your own personality preferences in the four areas of Energy, Perception, Decision-Making, and Orientation of your environment. After scoring yourself, repeat the exercise and answer how you think your manager would respond.

Energy: How You Recharge and Focus Your Attention

Extroversion	Introversion
☐ Devote more energy toward the outer world, focusing energy and attention to objects and people in the environment	☐ Devote more energy toward the inner world, focusing attention on clarity of thoughts, ideas, impressions
☐ Prefer group settings	☐ Prefer individual or small-group settings
☐ Like expanding your social circle and sphere of friends	☐ Carefully consider adding new friends due to the time and energy commitment of maintaining deep relationships
☐ Energized by starting and engaging in conversation; mingle easily with strangers	☐ Find it draining to keep the conversation going; small talk with strangers is taxing
☐ Process thoughts by thinking out loud; often have a quick response or witty comeback	☐ Process thoughts internally before speaking; often think of the perfect response hours later
☐ Active, enthusiastic, energetic, animated	☐ Reflective, calm demeanor, understated
☐ Enjoy entertainment that involves action	☐ Enjoy entertainment that sparks mental stimulation

☐ Prefer variety in workday; dislike working on one thing for a long time, especially if on their own

☐ Enjoy the spotlight

☐ Prefer to have a breadth of interests

☐ Enjoy working on one thing for a long time

☐ Happy to work behind the scenes

☐ Prefer to have a depth of understanding about a few interests

___ Total checkmarks for Extroversion column

___ Total checkmarks for Introversion column

Circle the preference that received the most checkmarks (if there is a tie, select Introversion):   Extroversion (E) or Introversion (I)

Perception: How You Take In Information

Sensing

☐ Trust information you can take in through your five senses

☐ Enjoy details and concrete, physical data

iNtuiting

☐ Trust information you can take in through inspiration, inference, impressions

☐ Enjoy abstract ideas and meanings

(continued)

(continued)

Sensing	iNtuiting
☐ Use precise, literal language; give detailed explanations	☐ Use general, figurative language; speak in metaphors and analogies
☐ Present or take in information in a step-by-step, sequential fashion	☐ Present or take in information tangentially
☐ Are pragmatic and results-oriented	☐ Are conceptual and idea-oriented
☐ Hands-on; trust experience	☐ Theoretical; trust ideas
☐ Realist, "what-is" perspective	☐ Visionary, "what-if" perspective
☐ Past or present, "here-and-now" orientation	☐ Future orientation
☐ See facts and details before seeing underlying patterns or whole concepts	☐ See behind-the-scenes before seeing individual facts and details
_____ Total checkmarks for Sensing column	_____ Total checkmarks for iNtuiting column

Circle the preference that received the most checkmarks (if there is a tie, select iNtuiting): Sensing (S) or iNtuiting (N)

Judging: How You Make Decisions

Thinking	Feeling
☐ Base decisions on logic and reasoning	☐ Base decisions on personal or social values
☐ Focus on analysis and objectivity	☐ Focus on people and harmony
☐ Deem it more important to be truthful than tactful	☐ Deem it important to be tactful as well as truthful
☐ Prefer objective, analytical presentation of facts	☐ May sense that your or others' feelings are not being valued when discussion centers on an objective, analytical presentation of facts
☐ Value fair treatment for everyone, with a one-standard-for-all philosophy	☐ Evaluate situations based on the individual, with an exception-to-the-rule viewpoint
☐ Tend to be critical; point out flaws	☐ Easily show appreciation to others; overlook others' flaws
☐ Detached, aloof; process-oriented	☐ Connected to people; people are integral to the process
☐ Often oblivious to others' feelings	☐ May be viewed as overly accommodating or overemotional

(continued)

(continued)

Thinking

- ☐ Facts drive decisions
- ☐ Make tough decisions despite any negative personal reactions

_____ Total checkmarks for Thinking column

Feeling

- ☐ Impact on others factors heavily into decisions
- ☐ Tender; effect of a decision on others can be more important than logic

_____ Total checkmarks for Feeling column

Circle the preference that received the most checkmarks (if there is a tie, select Feeling): Thinking (T) or Feeling (F)

Orientation: How You Orient Your Outer World

Judging

- ☐ Prefer a planned, organized, systematic approach to life
- ☐ Prefer to have things settled
- ☐ Formal and orderly; efficient
- ☐ Like expectations to be clearly defined
- ☐ Make lists, enjoy completing a task on time or early

Perceiving

- ☐ Prefer a spontaneous, flexible approach to life
- ☐ Prefer to leave things open
- ☐ Informal and easygoing; casual
- ☐ Are comfortable with ambiguity
- ☐ Starting the task is fun; finishing a task on time is optional

❏ Prefer to take in only the amount of information necessary to make a decision

❏ Start early to reduce stress of deadline pressure

❏ Let's get this done

❏ Enjoy organization; apply procedures to help structure task

❏ Decide quickly on goals and stay the course in achieving them

_____ Total checkmarks for Judging column

❏ Remain open to new information as long as possible in order to miss nothing that might be important

❏ Do most creative work when under deadline pressure

❏ Let's wait and see

❏ Enjoy variety and diversity; procedures can impede creativity

❏ Change goals when made aware of new information

_____ Total checkmarks for Perceiving column

Circle the preference that received the most checkmarks (if there is a tie, select Perceiving): Judging (J) or Perceiving (P)

Write your preferences for each of the four scales in the blanks on the following page.

MY PREFERENCES

Energy (Extroversion or Introversion): _____

Perception (Sensing or iNtuiting): _____

Judgment (Thinking or Feeling): _____

Orientation (Judging or Perceiving): _____

Identifying your individual preferences for energy, perception, judgment, and orientation is only the first step in understanding type. Together these four preferences mesh to create a richly complex personality type, which can best be understood by completing the MBTI® (or, for career purposes, the MBTI® Career Report). If you have not had the opportunity to take this assessment, I encourage you to do so. The results will enable you to target tasks that you find interesting and express your preferences on the job, which is like cycling with the wind at your back rather than in your face. You will need to work with an individual who is specially qualified to administer the MBTI® assessment (many career coaches and counselors possess this qualification—ask your career coach or counselor if they are MBTI®-Qualified). Alternatively, you can use an assessment similar to the MBTI called The Keirsey™ Temperament Sorter®-II available at www.advisorteam.com, which has both a career and corporate temperament report. Opt for the career report for insights into career choice or the corporate report for insights into how to communicate better with managers and team members.

Position Proposal and Resume Samples

Proof of performance is a requirement in persuading management to grant you new responsibilities. That proof might take the form of a position proposal that shows the scope of responsibilities and return on investment you can generate. Even when a position proposal is not necessary, you'll very likely need an internal resume or other document that highlights your contributions. Following are examples of both.

Position Proposal

This proposal for a new IS Human Capital Development Program (to be managed by the employee submitting the proposal) is linked to the mission, vision, and goals of the organization. It includes key objectives/outcomes, program benefits, and key deliverables, as well as financial projections on costs that could potentially be alleviated as a result of the program.

THE GREAT LAKES HEART INSTITUTE

Holding the Keys to Heart Health

Proposal for
IS Human Capital Development Program

Submitted by James Parker, MSN, Ed.D.
Information Systems Program

February 10, 20XX

Figure D.1: Position proposal for a new IS Human Capital Development Program.

Goal

The focus of this proposal is to establish an IS Human Capital Development (HCD) Program that incorporates the mission, vision, goals, and strategies of the Great Lakes Heart Institute to provide the support mechanisms necessary to create a learning and mentoring organization for all employees.

Business Needs

> ➢ Coordinated efforts to identify and establish core competencies for key roles to serve as quality standards for hiring, employee professional growth and development, retention, and reward.
> ➢ Centralized location for collaborative educational programming that incorporates existing internal and external training opportunities with vendors and IT/IS programs.
> ➢ Collaborative platform to work with directors and managers to incorporate development/mentoring goals and plans into employee evaluations.
> ➢ Communication and coordination with local IT/IS programs (technical schools, colleges, and universities) to establish internships and recruitment opportunities.
> ➢ Instill cultural sensitivity and a spirit of inclusion in the workforce through diversity training.
> ➢ Incorporate activities of the Institute for Healthcare Excellence, Human Resources, Internal Communications, and the Office of Institutional Diversity to create a comprehensive approach to becoming an employer of choice.

Anticipated Objectives/Outcomes

> ➢ Key roles will be identified for initial program focus that will have identified baseline quality standards for hiring, employee growth, and retention.
> ➢ The IS HCD will provide a collaborative location for all employee educational and training opportunities.
> ➢ The IS HCD will work with and assist IS directors and managers to incorporate professional development/mentoring goals and plans into employee evaluations.
> ➢ The IS HCD will establish formal and informal relationships with local IT/IS programs (technical schools, colleges, and universities) to establish internships and recruitment opportunities.
> ➢ The IS HCD will work with the Institute for Healthcare Excellence, Human Resources, Internal Communications, and the Office of Institutional Diversity to assess current deficiencies and create a comprehensive approach that will lead to the IS Division becoming an employer of choice within the IS/IT community.

Program Benefits and ROI

> ➢ Improved skills/competency quality of retained and hired staff
> ➢ Established clear role/position competencies (of designated roles)
> ➢ Established career advancement pathways—internal (program/department) and external (GLHI)
> ➢ Baseline Employee Development Plans for key roles (as identified by the needs assessment)

> Working relationships with local IS/IT program for internships and recruitment
> Resource coordination to meet GLHI strategic plan for cultural sensitivity and inclusion
> Improved employee job satisfaction
> Decreased employee turnover
> Phased implementation approach to validate program incremental successes
> Centralized location for collaborative educational programming to improve employee access to institutional resources (esp. HR Employee Development programming)

Other Considerations

> Coordination of IS Div/Dept Orientation
> Coordination of work/life program

Key Program Infrastructure Tasks and Deliverables

> Collaborative program needs assessment (Directors/Managers/Staff)
> Assessment of current cultural deficiencies and strategies to mitigate HCD Program SWOT Analysis
> Written agreements with local IS/IT programs for internships
> Competitive review of similar programs
> Proposed staff and support roles
> Proposed phased budget
> Key metrics for program evaluation
> Resource needs analysis (staff, software, and equipment)
> Risk Analysis
> Phased program implementation outline
> Establish ROI metrics for turnover (benchmarking and target goals to include, but not limited to) 5-year historical
  - Division/Department turnover by role
  - Employee satisfaction survey results
  - Associated turnover costs (see table depicting cost for nurses only; this number will be significantly higher when calculating other positions)

Our current turnover % for registered nurses:	23.33%
Average wage rate for this position:	$4,750/mo
Plus cost percentage of benefits:	35%
Total compensation for position:	$76,950
Total turnover cost for registered nurses:	$538,650
Replacement hiring costs, approximately 30%:	$161,595
Training new hire costs, estimated at 20%:	$107,730
Lost productivity and lost business cost, estimated at 10%:	$53,865
Total Expenses (Potential Savings to Organization):	**$861,840**

Before-and-After Resume Samples

Paul had been taken for granted at his current employer and was not perceived as a strong candidate for promotion. The "After" version of his resume was part of his rebranding initiative to be seen as an Operations Leader, Process Change Agent, and Employee Engagement Specialist (note those terms near the top of the resume and again under Professional Experience). The Career Highlights section emphasizes his most significant career accomplishments, which refreshes his current employer's awareness of his impressive track record. Numbers-driven accomplishments were included for his prior positions.

Paul Silverly

543 Brook Road
Chicago, IL 30507
(555) 555-5432 Cell
paul_silverly@email.com

Objective   To maximize career growth through experienced gained in the finance and mortgage industries.

Professional Experience

March 2005 - Present   ***Tops Mortgage Company***
Operations Manager
Manage 4 senior mortgage specialists and 8 outsourced sales specialists.

November 2003 – February 2005   ***SE Mortgage Solutions***
Portfolio Manager
Manage the acquisition and future liquidation of all manufactured inventory. Identification and enactment of most profitable case-by-case scenario is vital to the stability of the interim lending company. Manage the process of foreclosure, refurbishment and resale of all manufactured interim construction foreclosure portfolio. Manage analysis of varying forms of liquidation and short/long term profitability to parent company. Manage the completion of construction and sales of foreclosed manufactured home subdivisions.

August 2002 – October 2003   ***Bellwater Residential Homes***
Vice President - Construction Loan

- Initiated via investor contacts a new lending entity to enhance manufactured home construction lending opportunities to local retailers.
- Acted as liaison between retailer entity and manufactured lenders.

March 1994 – July 2002   ***Fi-Co Finance Company***
Senior Underwriter (1999-2002)

- Underwriter for one of the nation's largest residential lenders.
- Managed staff of 6 loan processors and 2 underwriters.
- Number one originating region in country 2 years.

Business Development Manager (1996-1999)`

- Developed lender client relationships for the Great Lakes Region of company.
- Manager of customer lender relation program.
- Managed staff of 3 customer service representatives tasked with improving customer lender relations.

Direct Marketing Representative (1994-1996)

- Developed new lending program to enhance after market resale of manufactured housing.
- Initiated consumer, retailer, broker program to market consumer-to-consumer lending program.
- Managed staff of 3 loan representatives and 2 marketing representatives.

Education   *1987-1991*   ***University of Chicago***
Bachelor Business Administration

- Performance-Driven Leadership

Community Service   Vice President of Boys Soccer Inc.; Member, High School Athletic Booster Club

Figure D.2: Paul's "Before" resume.

PAUL SILVERLY

Office: 555-555-4321   paul_silverly@topsmortage.com   Mobile: 555-555-5432

MORTGAGE OPERATIONS MANAGEMENT

Operations Leader • Process Change Agent • Employee Engagement Specialist

CAREER HIGHLIGHTS

- **Tops Mortgage Company:** Assembled and led team that significantly exceeded revenue goals, with a *47% overall increase in less than two years.*
- **SE Mortgage Solutions:** As Portfolio Manager, *delivered $16 million savings* to company through rapid disposition of foreclosure/abandonment inventory.
- **Bellwater Residential Homes:** As VP of Construction Loans, *exceeded revenue goals by $684,000*, more than tripling projected growth rate.
- **FI–Co Finance Company:** As Senior Underwriter, delivered performance as *#1 originating region in the country* for 3 consecutive years—a first for the region.
- **Summit Builders:** Land Financial Analyst during Summit's aggressive growth phase, where it grew from the area's #10 to #2 homebuilder. Developed a cash-flow predictor to analyze profitability of new purchases that was used for decision-making at the executive level.

PROFESSIONAL EXPERIENCE

OPERATIONS MANAGER—SALES   TOPS MORTGAGE COMPANY, Chicago, IL (March 2005-Present)

Manager of staff consisting of 4 senior mortgage specialists and 8 outsourced sales specialists.

Operations Leadership—Member of team that achieved the following successes:

- Provided leadership to team that significantly grew loan volume, with a 27% increase in year 1 and a 20% increase in year 2.
- Awarded the Tops Achievement Award in first year as manager for creation and execution of new campaign— reduced pre-list inventory by 27% in 4 months.
- Tenured manager on operations team who achieved "exceeds expectations" in all categories. Team achieved successes in three major metrics never before achieved simultaneously.

Process Change—Contributed to several firsts for the organization:

- Leader of team for the business process reengineering … reduced disposition cycle time 10-20 days through system enhancement that provides ability to upload offers.
- Manager of outsourced sales staff that reduced cycle for list to contract by 7 days … accomplished without negatively impacting recovery … recognized by senior management as a first for operations.
- Created numerous reports to monitor exceptions to timelines across each function of operations. Impacts include a reduction of portfolio cycle time of 30% in year 1 and 29% in year 2, including a historic low of 46% in August of this year.

Staff Development/Employee Engagement—

- Mentored Mortgage Technician who earned promotion to Sales Specialist.
- Served on inaugural Multi-Family Operations Strategic Team, which was cited for improving results of employee productivity survey.
- In 360 feedback from staff to director, cited as a strong manager. In feedback from other staff, requested as future manager. (continued)

543 Brook Road · Chicago, IL 30507 · Office: 555-555-4321 · Mobile: 555-555-5432 · paul_silverly@topsmortage.com

Figure D.3: Paul's "After" resume.   *(continued)*

(continued)

PAUL SILVERLY

Office: 555-555-4321   paul_silverly@topsmortgage.com   Mobile: 555-555-5432

PROFESSIONAL EXPERIENCE (continued)

PORTFOLIO MANAGER   SE MORTGAGE SOLUTIONS, Chicago, IL (11/03-2/05)

Recruited as consultant to mitigate losses and manage disposition of foreclosure inventory (several hundred manufactured properties scattered throughout the Northeast and Midwest). Identified root causes and implemented process change to prevent reoccurrence of situation. Trained and supervised staff in curative title processes, working with entities in multiple states. Managed marketing, sales, and closing of properties.

- Delivered $9 million in savings and reduced net forecasted loss of $2.4 million for this hard-money lender.

- Exceeded goal of placing 55% of loans with new borrower or selling collateral, turning 90% of loans.

- Reduced fallout on overall loan portfolio from 42% to 8%.

VICE PRESIDENT, CONSTRUCTION LOANS   BELLWATER RESIDENTIAL HOMES, Chicago, IL (8/02-10/03)

Initiated via investor contacts a new lending entity to enhance single-family construction lending opportunities to local retailers. Managed startup and ongoing operations of division.

- Grew production from 80 to 138 sales per year, surpassing target of a 25% increase with a 69% actual growth rate.

- Delivered more than $1.04 million in additional revenue, exceeding projected revenue by $684,000.

SENIOR UNDERWRITER   FI-CO FINANCE COMPANY, Chicago, IL (3/94-7/02)

Managed staff of 6 loan processors and 2 underwriters for Fi-Co, one of the nation's largest residential lenders.

- Grew monthly loan volume from 124 to 171, with a net gain of $45 million for the region's annual results.

- Improved ranking from #3 to #1-producing region in the country during two years as Senior Underwriter.

- Promoted through positions as Business Development Representative (1995-1997) and Direct Marketing Manager (1998-1999).

PRIOR EXPERIENCE: Began real estate career as Land Financial Analyst with Summit Builders (9/92-1/95). Created processes and tools to help accommodate a nearly tenfold increase in annual growth.

EDUCATION & CONTINUING PROFESSIONAL DEVELOPMENT

Bachelor of Business Administration, Finance—University of Chicago

Tops Mortgage Company Internal and External Training (partial list)
- **Leadership:** Writing Performance Reviews for Managers; Leadership
- **Mortgage Trends:** Lending in Emerging Markets; Trends in the Industry
- **Expanding market** training through convention attendance.

543 Brook Road · Chicago, IL 30507 · Office: 555-555-4321 · Mobile: 555-555-5432 · paul_silverly@topsmortage.com

25-Point Communication Check

To better gauge your listening and communication skills, take this "25-Point Communication Check." Complete the inventory yourself and then get a third-party perspective by asking a trusted friend or colleague to also rate you.

In business settings, I normally…

1. Am complimented for being a good listener.	Seldom	Occasionally	Often	Habitually
2. Allow others to finish their statements before responding.	Seldom	Occasionally	Often	Habitually
3. Allow give-and-take to conversations, where I listen as much as and usually more than I speak.	Seldom	Occasionally	Often	Habitually
4. Remain open to the listener's message rather than assume what I want to hear.	Seldom	Occasionally	Often	Habitually
5. Read between the lines, considering the speaker's values, priorities, and needs.	Seldom	Occasionally	Often	Habitually
6. Avoid thoughts of "right-ness"…that my way of thinking is right or better than the speaker's.	Seldom	Occasionally	Often	Habitually
7. Am respectful of and open to new ideas, not allowing differences in political, social, or religious beliefs to distract me from what the speaker is saying.	Seldom	Occasionally	Often	Habitually

8. Look past the irritation to the need when a speaker expresses emotions such as anger or frustration.	Seldom	Occasionally	Often	Habitually
9. Ignore verbal distractions (such as incorrect grammar, generational differences in language, regional accents, or profanity).	Seldom	Occasionally	Often	Habitually
10. Pay attention to body language and tonality to help me get the gist of the speaker's feelings.	Seldom	Occasionally	Often	Habitually
11. Remain fully "present" for the speaker—attentive, interested, curious, and interactive.	Seldom	Occasionally	Often	Habitually
12. Avoid multitasking, such as watching some other activity in the room, reviewing e-mail, clearing my desk, and so on.	Seldom	Occasionally	Often	Habitually
13. Listen for clues on how a speaker prefers to take in information (sequentially/ tangibly vs. intuitively/ conceptually).	Seldom	Occasionally	Often	Habitually
14. Listen for clues on how a speaker prefers to make decisions (from a thinking/ rational perspective vs. a feeling/ human-effect perspective).	Seldom	Occasionally	Often	Habitually
15. Keep emotions in check when listening and do not allow emotions to drive my responses.	Seldom	Occasionally	Often	Habitually
16. Use appropriate eye contact and body language when listening.	Seldom	Occasionally	Often	Habitually
17. Use appropriate eye contact, facial animation, and body language when speaking.	Seldom	Occasionally	Often	Habitually

18. Do not steer the conversation toward my agenda or make it all about me.	Seldom	Occasionally	Often	Habitually
19. Ask the speaker to clarify if I am not clear on what was said.	Seldom	Occasionally	Often	Habitually
20. Outline the speaker's key points to be certain I understand the message.	Seldom	Occasionally	Often	Habitually
21. Consider whether my response will be relevant to the speaker (in other words, avoid too many extraneous details or too many stories about myself).	Seldom	Occasionally	Often	Habitually
22. Consider the best approach to sharing, so that the speaker finds personal benefit in my response.	Seldom	Occasionally	Often	Habitually
23. Am accurate and concise in my responses.	Seldom	Occasionally	Often	Habitually
24. Keep the conversation focused so that important issues are prioritized.	Seldom	Occasionally	Often	Habitually
25. Respect and appreciate others prior to expecting the same for myself.	Seldom	Occasionally	Often	Habitually

Appendix F

Success Story Contributors

The following Certified Career Management Coaches (CCMC) from Career Coach Academy (www.CareerCoachAcademy.com) and members of Career Masters Institute (www.cminstitute.com) contributed to the success stories found in chapter 7. Please feel free to contact them if you need additional help with your promotion plan.

Clay Cerny, Ph.D.
AAA Targeted Writing & Coaching Services
Chicago, Illinois
Phone: (773) 907-8660
E-mail: claycerny2@msn.com
www.aaatargeted.com

Jane Cranston
ExecutiveCoachNY.com
New York, New York
Phone: (212) 628-5280
E-mail: jane@executivecoachny.com
www.ExecutiveCoachNY.com

George Dutch, CCM, CMF, JCTC
JobJoy
Ottawa, Ontario, Canada
Phone: (613) 563-0584
E-mail: george@jobjoy.com
www.jobjoy.com

Dale R. Kurow, M.S.
New York, New York
Phone: (212) 787-6097
E-mail: dkurow@nyc.rr.com
www.dalekurow.com

Bobbie LaPorte, MBA
RAL & Associates
San Francisco, California
Phone: (415) 242-1766
E-mail: blaporte@sbcglobal.net

Sharon McCormick, M.S., MCC, NCCC, NCC, CPRW
Sharon McCormick Career &
   Vocational Consulting Services, LLC
St. Petersburg, Florida
Phone: (727) 824-7805
E-mail: career1@ij.net

Marcia Merrill, M.Ed., M.S., CCMC, JCTC
Marcia Merrill, LLC dba eCareerCorner.com
Baltimore, Maryland
Phone: (410) 467-0811
E-mail: marcia@ecareercorner.com
www.eCareerCorner.com

Barb Poole, B.S., CCMC, CPRW, CERW
Hire Imaging
St. Cloud, Minnesota
Phone: (320) 253-0975
E-mail: barb@hireimaging.com
www.hireimaging.com

Judit Price, M.S., CCM, CDFI, IJCTC, CPRW, CCM
Berke & Price Associates
Chelmsford, Massachusetts
Phone: (978) 256-0482
E-mail: jprice@careercampaign.com
www.careercampaign.com

Beth Woodworth, M.S., JCTC, CRPCC, CDFI, CAC, GFMF, CWDP
Job Training Center of Tehama
   County
Red Bluff, California
Phone: (530) 529-7000, ext. 122
E-mail: bwoodworth@ncen.org
www.jobtrainingcenter.org

Heather T. Zeng, Ph.D.
Fremont, California
Phone: (786) 246-6232
Fax: (866) 708-7016
E-mail: heatherzeng@aol.com

Index

A

abusive bosses, 59

action steps of game plan, 31–33

Aesthetic needs, 5

agendas, in T.A.L.K., 79–101

alignment with company values, 62–63

America's Career InfoNet Web site, 11

appearance, problems with (roadblock to promotion), 123–125

arms (in body language), 93

articulation, 102

assertiveness, 103

assessments
  list of, 180–184
  self-scoring personality type assessment, 189–196
  25-Point Communication Check, 205–207

attitude toward work, 7

auditory learning style, 90–91

automotive industry, 10

B

Bar-On, Reuven, 6

BarOn EQ-i assessment, 180

Before-After-and-Beyond Position Description
  creating, 94–96
  table, 94

Bellah, Robert, 63

Belonging and Love needs, 4

Berens, Linda V., 185

Beta Research Corporation, 53–54

Birkman Method assessment, 180

Bitschenauer, Kathy, 28, 179

body language, 92–93, 105

bonuses, 139

Book, Howard E., 185

branding, 28–30, 50–52

Branton, Nancy, 48, 56

Briggs, Katharine, 87

Buckingham, Marcus, 185

budget considerations, in salary negotiations, 145–146

C

callings, defined, 63

Career Coach Academy, 149, 209

career coaches, 26–27

Career Distinction: Stand Out by Building Your Brand, 50

Career Leader assessment, 180

career management, 48–50

Career "Master F.I.T." Worksheet, 18–19

Career Masters Institute, 149, 209

career needs, 3–6

Career Needs worksheet, 5–6

career success, factors in, 47–63

careers
  defined, 63
  fit for, 15–19

Careerstrength assessment, 181

case studies. *See* success stories

Cerny, Clay, 154, 209

Certified Career Management Coaches (CCMC), 149, 209

challenge, attitude toward (characteristic of resiliency), 113

character (characteristic of promotability), 8

Clifton, Donald O., 185

Clifton StrengthsFinder assessment, 181

clothing (roadblock to promotion), 123–125

coachable (characteristic of promotability), 10

Cognitive needs, 5

COLA (Cost Of Living Adjustment), 139

collaboration, in salary negotiations, 142

commitment
  characteristic of promotability, 10
  characteristic of resiliency, 113